Y0-BRW-356

"Not I, But the Wind..."

"NOT I, BUT THE WIND..."

BY FRIEDA LAWRENCE

geb. Freiin von Richthofen

1934

THE VIKING PRESS · NEW YORK

Printed in U. S. A. Distributed in Canada by the Macmillan Companv of Canada, Ltd.

FIRST TRADE EDITION PUBLISHED IN OCTOBER 1934

Foreword

It was still cold last night, though it is the middle of May.

Here the ranch, with the Sangre de Cristo mountain range behind it to the northeast, slopes to the desert. The big pine trees stand like dark sentinels in the night at the edge of the twenty acre alfalfa field. Beyond them floats the desert. You can see far. A few lights twinkle at Ranchos de Taos. A shepherd's fire glows. All is covered by an enormous sky full of stars, stars that hang in the pine trees, in Lawrence's big tree with his phœnix on it that the Brett painted, stars that lean on the edge of the mountains, stars twinkling out of the Milky Way. It is so still. Only stars, nothing but stars.

This morning early there was still ice on the edge of the irrigation ditch from the Gallina Canyon. There is such a rush of water. The ice is melting high up in the mountains and the water sings through one's blood.

But now, about midday, it is warm. The desert below circles in rings of shadow and sunshine. The alfalfa field is green, during these last days of sunshine it has turned green.

I am in the little cabin that Lawrence built with the Indians. I sit in the chair that he made with the "petit point" canvas that we bought in the Rue de la Paix in Paris and that I embroidered. It took me a long time, and when I got bored, he did a bit.

It is a nice chair, although a bit rough, carved as it was with only a penknife.

So here I sit and try to write.

I did not want to write this book. I wanted to give Lawrence my silence. Would he have wanted me to write it? Would he have jeered at me as one of those intellectual females whom he disliked so much? Is it any use, my writing?

Do I want to blow my own trumpet? Yes, I do. But will it have a clear rousing sound or will it be a bit wheezy and out of tune? Can I hear the real song of our life, the motifs gay, bold, sad, terrible, or can't I?

After all, this is my book, that I am writing. Do I understand anything at all or am I only recording unliving dull facts?

Is it a genuine necessity for me to write or has Lawrence said all a million times better than I could? Will this, that costs me so much, be of any use, any pleasure to anybody else? Will others who come after learn from our life, take from it the good and avoid our mistakes? . . . I wonder. . . .

Anyhow, I will try to write as honestly as I can. Lies are all very well in their place but the truth seems to me so much more interesting and proud, but truth is not so easily conquered, there is always more of it, like a bottomless pit is truth. It was a long fight for Lawrence and me to get at some truth between us; it was a hard life with him, but a wonderful one. Stark and bare, without trimmings and frills. But a few realities remained, a lasting truth triumphed.

Whatever happened on the surface of everyday life, there blossomed the certainty of the unalterable bond between us, and of the everpresent wonder of all the world around us.

We had so many battles to fight out, so much to get rid of, so much to surpass. We were both good fighters.

There was the ordinary man-and-woman fight between us,

to keep the balance, not to trespass, not to topple over. The balance in a human relationship was one of Lawrence's chief themes. He felt that each should keep intact his own integrity and isolation, yet at the same time preserve a mutual bond like the north and south poles which between them enclose the world.

Then there was the class war. We came from different worlds. We both had to reach beyond our class, to be reborn into the essence of our individual beings, the essence that is so much deeper than any class distinction.

Then beyond class there was the difference in race, to cross over to each other. He, the Englishman, Puritan, stern and uncompromising, so highly conscious and responsible; I, the German, with my vagueness and uncertainty, drifting along.

Only the fierce common desire to create a new kind of life, this was all that could make us truly meet.

As for pretending to understand Lawrence or to explain him, I am neither so impertinent nor such a fool. We are so much more than we understand. Understanding is such a little part of us, there is so much in us of unexplored territory that understanding can never grasp. As Lawrence and I were adventurers by nature, we explored.

I only know that I felt the wonder of him always. Sometimes it overwhelmed me, it knocked out all my consciousness as if a flame had burnt me up. I remained in awe and wonder.

Sometimes I hated him and held him off as if he were the devil himself. At other times I took him as you take the weather. Here's a spring day, glorious sunshine, what a joy! Then another day—alas! all is changed: it is chilly and it rains and I wish, how I wish, it were sunny again.

I learned that a genius contains the whole gamut of human

emotions, from highest to lowest. I learned that a man must be himself, bad or good at any price.

Life and emotions change in us. We are not pictures, "Patiences on monuments"; anyhow Lawrence wasn't, nor I either. Ours was not just a love affair, just as his writing was not just writing as a profession.

His love wiped out all my shames and inhibitions, the failures and the miseries of my past. He made me new and fresh, that I might live freely and lightly as a bird. He fought for the liberty of my being, and won. Just as in his writings he tried, with his fierce and responsible love for his fellowmen, to free them of the stale old past, and take the load of all the centuries of dead thought and feeling on himself.

Will the world gain from him as I did? I hope so, in the long run.

Contents

Illustrations

"Not I, But the Wind..."

⸙

We Meet

As I look back now it surprises me that Lawrence could have loved me at first sight as he did. I hardly think I could have been a very lovable woman at the time. I was thirty-one and had three children. My marriage seemed a success. I had all a woman can reasonably ask. Yet there I was, all "smock ravelled," to use one of Lawrence's phrases.

I had just met a remarkable disciple of Freud and was full of undigested theories. This friend did a lot for me. I was living like a somnambulist in a conventional set life and he awakened the consciousness of my own proper self.

Being born and reborn is no joke, and being born into your own intrinsic self, that separates and singles you out from all the rest—it's a painful process.

When people talk about sex, I don't know what they mean—as if sex hopped about by itself like a frog, as if it had no relation to the rest of living, one's growth, one's ripening. What people mean by sex will always remain incomprehensible to me, but I am thankful to say sex is a mystery to me.

Theories applied to life aren't any use. Fanatically I believed that if only sex were "free" the world would straightaway turn into a paradise. I suffered and struggled at outs with society, and felt absolutely isolated. The process left me unbalanced. I felt alone. What could I do, when there were so many millions who thought differently from me? But I couldn't give in, I couldn't submit. It wasn't that I felt hostile, only different. I could not accept society. And then Lawrence came. It was an April day in 1912. He came for lunch, to see my husband about a lectureship at a German University. Lawrence was also at a critical period of his life just then. The death of his mother had shaken the foundations of his health for a second time. He had given up his post as a schoolmaster at Croydon. He had done with his past life.

I see him before me as he entered the house. A long thin figure, quick straight legs, light, sure movements. He seemed so obviously simple. Yet he arrested my attention. There was something more than met the eye. What kind of a bird was this?

The half-hour before lunch the two of us talked in my room, French windows open, curtains fluttering in the spring wind, my children playing on the lawn.

He said he had finished with his attempts at knowing women. I was amazed at the way he fiercely denounced them. I had never before heard anything like it. I laughed, yet I could tell he had tried very hard, and had cared. We talked about Œdipus and understanding leaped through our words.

After leaving, that night, he walked all the way to his home. It was a walk of at least five hours. Soon afterwards he wrote to me: "You are the most wonderful woman in all England."

I wrote back: "You don't know many women in England, how do you know?" He told me, the second time we met: "You are quite unaware of your husband, you take no notice of him." I disliked the directness of this criticism.

He came on Easter Sunday. It was a bright, sunny day. The children were in the garden hunting for Easter eggs.

The maids were out and I wanted to make some tea. I tried to turn on the gas but didn't know how. Lawrence be-

FRIEDA LAWRENCE

came cross at such ignorance. Such a direct critic! It was something my High and Mightiness was very little accustomed to.

Yet Lawrence really understood me. From the first he saw through me like glass, saw how hard I was trying to keep up a cheerful front. I thought it was so despicable and unproud and unclean to be miserable, but he saw through my hard bright shell.

What I cannot understand is how he could have loved me and wanted me at that time. I certainly did have what he called "sex in the head"; a theory of loving men. My real self was frightened and shrank from contact like a wild thing.

So our relationship developed.

One day we met at a station in Derbyshire. My two small girls were with us. We went for a long walk through the early-spring woods and fields. The children were running here and there as young creatures will.

We came to a small brook, a little stone bridge crossed it. Lawrence made the children some paper boats and put matches in them and let them float downstream under the bridge. Then he put daisies in the brook, and they floated down with their upturned faces. Crouched by the brook, playing there with the children, Lawrence forgot about me completely.

Suddenly I knew I loved him. He had touched a new tenderness in me. After that, things happened quickly.

He came to see me one Sunday. My husband was away and I said: "Stay the night with me." "No, I will not stay in your husband's house while he is away, but you must tell him the truth and we will go away together, because I love you."

I was frightened. I knew how terrible such a thing would be

for my husband, he had always trusted me. But a force stronger than myself made me deal him the blow. I left the next day. I left my son with his father, my two little girls I took to their grandparents in London. I said good-bye to them on Hampstead Heath, blind and blank with pain, dimly feeling I should never again live with them as I had done.

Lawrence met me at Charing Cross Station, to go away with him, never to leave him again.

He seemed to have lifted me body and soul out of all my past life. This young man of twenty-six had taken all my fate, all my destiny, into his hands. And we had known each other barely for six weeks. There had been nothing else for me to do but submit.

Going Away Together

We met at Charing Cross and crossed the grey channel sitting on some ropes, full of hope and agony. There was nothing but the grey sea, and the dark sky, and the throbbing of the ship, and ourselves.

We arrived at Metz where my father was having his fifty-years-of-service jubilee. Prewar Germany: the house was full of grandchildren and relatives, and I stayed in a hotel where Lawrence also stayed. It was a hectic time. Bands were playing in honour of my father, telegrams came flying from England. Lawrence was pulling me on one side, my children on the other. My mother wanted me to stay with her. My father, who loved me, said to me in great distress: "My child, what are you doing? I always thought you had so much sense. I know the world." I answered: "Yes, that may be, but you never knew the best." I meant to know the best.

There was a fair going on at Metz at the moment. I was walking with my sister Johanna through the booths of Turkish Delight, the serpentmen, the ladies in tights, all the pots and pans.

Johanna, or "Nusch," as we called her, was at the height of her beauty and elegance, and was the last word in "chic." Suddenly Lawrence appeared round a corner, looking odd, in a cap and raincoat. What will she think of him, I thought.

He spoke a few words to us and went away. To my surprise, Johanna said: "You can go with him. You can trust him."

At first nobody knew of Lawrence's presence except my sisters. One afternoon Lawrence and I were walking in the fortifications of Metz, when a sentinel touched Lawrence on the shoulder, suspecting him of being an English officer. I had to get my father's help to pull us out of the difficulty. Lo, the cat was out of the bag, and I took Lawrence home to tea.

He met my father only once, at our house. They looked at each other fiercely—my father, the pure aristocrat, Lawrence, the miner's son. My father, hostile, offered a cigarette to Lawrence. That night I dreamt that they had a fight, and that Lawrence defeated my father.

The strain of Metz proved too great for Lawrence and he left for the Rhineland. I stayed behind in Metz.

Here are some of Lawrence's letters, which show his side of our story up to that time.

EASTWOOD—TUESDAY

I feel so horrid and helpless. I know it all sickens you, and you are almost at the end of the tether. And what was decent yesterday will perhaps be frightfully indecent today. But it's like being ill: there's nothing to do but shut one's teeth and look at the wall and wait.

You say you're going to G . . . tomorrow. But even that is uncertain. And I must *know about the trains. What time are you going to Germany, what day, what hour, which railway, which class? Do tell me as soon as you can, or else what I can do? I will come any time you tell me—but let me know.*

You must be in an insane whirl in your mind. I feel helpless and rudderless, a stupid scattered fool. For goodness' sake tell me something, and something definite. I would do anything on earth for you, and I can do nothing. Yesterday I knew would be decent, but I don't like my feeling today—presentiment. I am afraid of something low, like an eel which bites out of the mud, and hangs on with its teeth. I feel as if I can't breathe while we're in England. I wish I could come and see you, or else you me.

D. H. LAWRENCE

QUEENS SQUARE,
EASTWOOD, NOTTS
2 MAY 1912

I shall get in Kings Cross tomorrow at 1:25. Will that do? You see I couldn't come today because I was waiting for the laundry and for some stuff from the tailor's. I had prepared for Friday, but Thursday was impossible. I am sorry if it makes things tiresome.

Will you meet me, or let somebody meet me, at King's Cross? Or else wire me very *early, what to do. It is harassing to be as we are.*

I have worried endlessly over you. Is that an insult? But I shan't get an easy breath till I see you. This time tomorrow, exactly, I shall be in London.

I hope you've got some money for yourself. I can muster only eleven pounds. A chap owes me twenty-five quid, but is in such a fix himself, I daren't bother him. At any rate, eleven pounds will take us to Metz, then I must rack my poor brains.

Oh Lord, I must say "making history," as Garnett puts it, isn't the most comfortable thing on earth. If I knew how things stood with you, I wouldn't care a damn. As it is, I eat my blessed heart out.

Till tomorrow, till tomorrow, till tomorrow (I nearly put à demain).

D. H. LAWRENCE

P.S. I haven't told anything to anybody. Lord, but I wonder how you are.

D. H. L.

METZ

Damn the rain! I suppose you won't go out while it continues heavily. I'll venture forth in a minute—9:15 already. I don't know where you live exactly—so if I can't find you I shall put this in number 4. That's the nearest I can get; is it right?

If I don't meet you, I suppose I shan't see you today, since this is the festive day. I don't mind. At least, I do, but I understand it can't be helped.

I shall go into the country if it'll keep a bit fine—shall be home here about 2:30, I suppose. I can work as soon as I like.

Let us go away from Metz. Tell Else I'm not cross. How should I be? You are the soul of good intention—how can one be cross with you? But I wish I had the management of our affairs.

Don't love me for things I'm not—but also don't tell me I'm mean. I wondered what had become of you this morning. Were you being wise and good and saving my health? You needn't. I'm not keen on coming to your place to lunch tomorrow—but I am in your hands—"into thine hand, O Lord, I commend," etc. I want you to do as you like, over little things such as my coming to your father's house. In oddments, your will is my will.

I love you—but I always have to bite my tongue before I can say it. It's only my Englishness.

Commend me to your sister. I lodge an appeal with her. I shall say to her—it's no good saying it to you—"Ayez pitié de moi."

No, I'm only teasing. It doesn't matter at all what happens—

or what doesn't *happen, that's more to the point—these few days. But if you put up your fingers, and count your days in Germany, and compare them with the days to follow in Nottingham, then you will see, you—(I don't mean it)—are selling sovereigns at a penny each. No,* you *are not doing it—but it's being done.*

Don't be hurt, or I shall—let me see—go into a monastery—this hotel is precious much like one already.

This is the last day I let you off—so make the most of it and be jolly.

TUESDAY—

Now I can't stand it any longer, I can't. For two hours I haven't moved a muscle—just sat and thought. I have written a letter to E. . . . You needn't, of course, send it. But you must say to him all I have said. No more dishonour, no more lies. Let them do their—silliest—but no more subterfuge, lying, dirt, fear. I feel as if it would strangle me. What is it all but procrastination. No, I can't bear it, because it's bad. I love you. Let us face anything, do anything, put up with anything. But this crawling under the mud I cannot bear.

I'm afraid I've got a fit of heroics. I've tried so hard to work —but I can't. This situation is round my chest like a cord. It mustn't *continue. I will go right away, if you like. I will stop in Metz till you get E . . .'s answer to the truth. But no, I won't utter or act or willingly let you utter or act, another single lie in the business.*

I'm not going to joke, I'm not going to laugh, I'm not going to make light of things for you. The situation tortures me too much. It's the situation, the situation I can't stand—no, and I won't. I love you too much.

Don't show this letter to either of your sisters—no. Let us be good. You are clean, but you dirty your feet. I'll sign myself as you call me—Mr. Lawrence.

Don't be miserable—if I didn't love you I wouldn't mind when you lied.

But I love you, and Lord, I pay for it.

HOTEL RHEINISCHER HOF, TRIER
8 MAY 1912

I am here—I have dined—it seems rather nice. The hotel is little—the man is proprietor, waiter, bureau, and everything else, apparently—speaks English and French and German quite sweetly—has evidently been in swell restaurants abroad —has an instinct for doing things decently, with just a touch of swank—is cheap—his wife (they're a youngish couple) draws the beer—it's awfully nice. The bedroom is two marks fifty per day, including breakfast—per person. That's no more than my room at the Deutscher Hof, and this is much nicer. It's on the second floor—two beds—rather decent. Now, you ought to be here, you ought to be here. Remember, you are to be my wife—see that they don't send you any letters, or only under cover to me. But you aren't here yet. I shall love Trier—it isn't a ghastly medley like Metz—new town, old town, barracks, barracks, cathedral, Montigny. This is nice, old, with trees down the town. I wish you were here. The valley all along coming is full of apple trees in blossom, pink puffs like the smoke of an explosion, and then bristling vine sticks, so that the hills are angry hedgehogs.

I love you so much. No doubt there'll be another dish of tragedy in the morning, and we've only enough money to run us a fortnight, and we don't know where the next will come from, but still I'm happy, I am happy. But I wish you were here. But you'll come, and it isn't Metz. Curse Metz.

They are all men in this hotel—business men. They are the connoisseurs of comfort and moderate price. Be sure men will get the best for the money. I think it'll be nice for you. You don't mind a masculine atmosphere, I know.

I begin to feel quite a man of the world. I ought, I suppose, with this wickedness of waiting for another man's wife in my heart. Never mind, in heaven there is no marriage nor giving in marriage.

I must hurry to post—it's getting late. Come early on Saturday morning. Ask the Black Hussy at Deutscher Hof if there are any letters for me. I love you—and Else—I do more than thank her. Love

D. H. LAWRENCE

Hotel Rheinischer Hof
Trier—Thursday

Another day nearly gone—it is just sunset. Trier is a nice town. This is a nice hotel. The man is a cocky little fellow, but good. He's lived in every country and swanks about his languages. He really speaks English nicely. He's about thirty-five, I should think. When I came in just now—it is sunset—he said, "You are tired?" It goes without saying I laughed. "A little bit," he added, quite gently. That amuses me. He would do what my men friends always want to do, look after me a bit in the trifling, physical matters.

I have written a newspaper article that nobody on earth will print, because it's too plain and straight. However, I don't care. And I've been a ripping walk—up a great steep hill nearly like a cliff, beyond the river. I will take you on Saturday—so nice: apple blossom everywhere, and the cuckoo, and brilliant beech trees. Beech leaves seem to rush *out in spring, with* éclat. *You can have coffee at a nice place, and look at the town, like a handful of cinders and rubbish thrown beside the river down below. Then there are the birds always. And I went past a Madonna stuck with flowers, beyond the hilltop, among all the folds and jumble of hills: pretty as heaven. And I smoked a pensive cigarette, and philosophized about love and life and battle, and you and me. And I thought of a theme for my next novel. And I forgot the German for matches, so I had to beg a light from a young priest, in French, and he held me the red end of his cigar. There are not so many soldiers here. I should never hate Trier. There are more priests than soldiers. Of the sort I've seen—not a bit Jesuitical—I prefer them. The cathedral is crazy: a grotto, not a cathedral, inside—baroque, baroque. The town is always pleasant, and the people.*

One more day, and you'll be here. Suddenly I see your chin. I love your chin. At this moment, I seem to love you, because you've got such a nice chin. Doesn't it seem ridiculous?

I must go down to supper. I am *tired. It was a long walk. And then the strain of these days. I dreamed E . . . was frantically furiously wild with me—I won't tell you the details —and then he calmed down, and I had to comfort him. I am a devil at dreaming. It's because I get up so late. One always dreams after seven a.m.*

The day is gone. I'll talk a bit to my waiter fellow, and post this. You will *come on Saturday? By Jove, if you don't! We shall always have to battle with* life, *so we'll never fight with each other, always help.*

Bis Samstag—ich liebe dich schwer.

D. H. LAWRENCE

Postcard with picture of Trier, Porta Nigra

Here is your Porta Nigra, that you have missed three times. I think I am quite clever. It is a weird and circuitous journey to Waldbröl—seven hours. Now I am at Niederlahnstein—Rechtrheinisch—having just come over from Coblentz! I go on to Troisdorf—ever heard of such places!—then to Hennef—and at last Waldbröl—four changes—umsteigen—seven hours' journey. But isn't the Mosel valley pretty? The Rhein is most awfully German. It makes me laugh. It looks fearfully fit for the theatre. Address me care of Frau Karl Krenkow, Waldbröl Rheinprovinz. Anything new and nasty happened? This is my *sentimental journey.*

Love

D. H. Lawrence

Postcard with picture of Trier, Basilica

Now, I am in Hennef—my last changing place. It is 8:30—and still an hour to wait. So I am sitting like a sad swain beside a nice, twittering little river, waiting for the twilight to drop, and my last train to come. I shan't get to Waldbröl till after 11:00—nine hours on the way—and that is the quickest it can be done. But it's a nice place, Hennef, nearly like England. It's getting dark. Now for the first time during today, my detachment leaves me, and I know I only love you. The rest is nothing at all. And the promise of life with you is all richness. Now I know.

D. H. Lawrence

Adr. Frau Karl Krenkow
Waldbröl—Rheinprovinz

It's really very nice here—Hannah is very bright and so decent with me. Her husband is "a very good man"—uninteresting. She never loved him—married him because she was thirty and time going by. Already she's quite fond of me—but do not mind, she is perfectly honourable—the last word of respectability. Then there is "Opar-O'pa"—how do you spell it?—Stülchen. He is seventy-three—a lovely old man—really a sweet disposition, and no fool. Now he is really lovable. It was Kermesse at one of the villages yesterday—Sunday—and we went to look. It was jolly. Onkel Stülchen bought us a Herz—a great heart of cake, covered with sugar, and sugar grapes, and sugar roses, and a bird, a dove—and three pieces of poetry. It's rather quaint. Strange, how deep symbolism is in your soil. Herr Stülchen brought up Hannah, since she was five years old. Her father was killed—or died awhile after the Franco-Prussian War. Now I am fond of him.

Here, I am so respectable, and so good—it is quite a rest. We are not dull. Hannah is really intelligent. We amuse ourselves a good deal with my German. In three months here I should know quite a lot.

It's a quiet, dead little village—miles from everywhere—rather pretty in a tame sort of way—a bit Englishy. Once they let me begin, I shall knock off quite a lot of work. There is that novel on my conscience.

I write in the morning, when one is wonderfully sane. Wald-

bröl is good for my health—it is cooler, more invigorating. Trier was like a perpetual Turkish bath. I like this air.

If you must go to England—must you?—go before I leave Waldbröl. Don't leave me stranded in some unearthly German town. How are you? I am not going to sound worried over you, because I am so a bit. You might write to me and tell me a few significant details. The tragedy will begin to slacken off from now, I think.

I wrote to you yesterday, but it wasn't a nice letter, so I didn't send it. Things are better, surely, and growing better—oh yes!

FRIEDA VON RICHTHOFEN

Waldbröl—Mittwoch

I have had all your three letters quite safely. We are coming on quickly now. Do tell me if you can what is E . . .'s final decision. He will get the divorce, I think, because of his thinking you ought to marry me. That is the result of my *letter to him. I will crow my little crow, in opposition to you. And then after six months, we will be married—will you? Soon we will go to Munich. But give us a little time. Let us get solid before we set up together. Waldbröl restores me to my decent sanity. Is Metz still bad for you–no? It will be better for me to stay here—shall I say till the end of next week. We must decide what we are going to do, very definitely. If I am to come to Munich next week, what are we going to live on? Can we scramble enough together to last us till my payments come in? I am not going to tell my people anything till you have the divorce. If we can go decently over the first three or four months—financially—I think* I *shall be able to keep us going for the rest. Never mind about the infant. If it should come, we will be glad, and stir ourselves to provide for it—and if it should not come, ever—I shall be sorry. I do not believe, when people love each other, in interfering there. It is wicked, according to my feeling. I want you to have children to me—I don't care how soon. I never thought I should have that definite desire. But you see, we must have a more or less stable foundation if we are going to run the risk of the responsibility of children—not the risk of children, but the risk of the responsibility.*

I think after a little while, I shall write to E . . . again. Perhaps he would correspond better with me.

Can't you feel how certainly I love you and how certainly we shall be married? Only let us wait just a short time, to get strong again. Two shaken, rather sick people together would be a bad start. A little waiting, let us have, because I love you. Or does the waiting make you worse?—no, not when it is only a time of preparation. Do you know, like the old knights, I seem to want a certain time to prepare myself—a sort of vigil with myself. Because it is a great thing for me to marry you, not a quick, passionate coming together. I know in my heart "here's my marriage." It feels rather terrible—because it is a great thing in my life—it is my life*—I am a bit awe-inspired—I want to get used to it. If you think it is fear and indecision, you wrong me. It is* you *who would hurry, who are undecided. It's the very strength and inevitability of the oncoming thing that makes me wait, to get in harmony with it. Dear God, I am marrying you, now, don't you see. It's a far greater thing than ever I knew. Give me till next weekend, at least. If you love me, you will understand.*

If I seem merely frightened and reluctant to you—you must forgive me.

I try, I will always try, when I write to you, to write the truth as near the mark as I can get it. It frets me, for fear you are disappointed in me, and for fear you are too much hurt. But you are strong when necessary.

You have got all myself—I don't even flirt—it would bore me very much—unless I got tipsy. It's a funny thing, to feel one's passion—sex desire—no longer a sort of wandering thing, but steady, and calm. I think, when one loves, one's very sex passion becomes calm, a steady sort of force, instead of a storm. Passion, that nearly drives one mad, is far away from real love. I am realizing things that I never thought to realize. Look at that poem I sent you—I would never write that to you. I shall love you all my life. That also is a new idea to me. But I believe it.

Auf Wiedersehen

D. H. Lawrence

Adr Herrn Karl Krenkow
Waldbröl—Rheinprovinz
14 May 1912

Yes, I got your letter later in the day—and your letter and E . . .'s and yours to Garnett, this morning. In E . . .'s, as in mine to E . . ., see the men combining in their freemasonry against you. It is very strange.

I will send your letter to Garnett. I enclose one of his to me. It will make you laugh.

With correcting proofs, and reading E . . .'s letter, I feel rather detached. Things are coming straight. When you got in London, and had to face that judge, it would make you ill. We are not callous enough to stand against the public, the whole mass of the world's disapprobation, in a sort of criminal dock. It destroys us, though we deny it. We are all off the balance. We are like spring scales that have been knocked about. We had better be still awhile, let ourselves come to rest.

Things are working out to their final state now. I did not do wrong in writing to E. . . . Do not write to my sister yet. When all is a "fait accompli" then we will tell her, because then it will be useless for her to do other than to accept.

I am very well, but, like you, I feel shaky. Shall we not leave our meeting till we are better? Here, in a little while, I shall be solid again. And if you must go to England, will you go to Munich first—so far? No, I don't want to be left alone in Munich. Let us have firm ground where we next go. Quakiness and uncertainty are the death of us. See, tell me exactly what you are going to do. Is the divorce coming off? Are you going to England at all? Are we going finally to pitch our camp in Munich? Are we going to have enough money to get along with? Have you settled anything definite with E . . . ?—One must be detached, impersonal, cold, and logical, when one is arranging affairs. We do not want another fleet of horrors attacking us when we are on a rather flimsy raft—lodging in a borrowed flat on borrowed money.

Look, my dear, now that the suspense is going over, we can wait even a bit religiously for one another. My next coming to you is solemn, intrinsically—I am solemn over it—not sad, oh no—but it is my marriage, after all, and a great thing—not a thing to be snatched and clumsily handled. I will not come to you unless it is safely, and firmly. When I have come, things shall not put us apart again. So we must wait and watch for the hour. Henceforth, dignity in our movements and our arrangements—no shufflings and underhandedness. And we must settle the money business. I will write to the publishers, if necessary, for a sub. I have got about £30 due in August—£24 due–and £25 more I am owed. Can we wait, or not, for that?

Now I shall do as I like, because you are not certain. Even if I stay in Waldbröl a month, I won't come till our affair is welded firm. I can wait a month—a year almost—for a sure thing. But an unsure thing is a horror to me.

I love you—and I am in earnest about it—and we are going to make a great—or, at least, a good life together. I'm not going to risk fret and harassment, which would spoil our intimacy, because of hasty forcing of affairs.

Don't think I love you less, in being like this. You will think *so, but it isn't true. The best man in me loves you. And I dread anything dragging our love down.*

Be definite, my dear; be detailed, be business-like. In our marriage, let us be business-like. The love is there—then let the common-sense match it.

Auf Wiedersehen

D. H. LAWRENCE

This poetry will come in next month's English. *I'm afraid you won't like it.*

D. H. L.

And I love you, and I am sorry it is so hard. But it is only a little while—then we will have a dead cert.

WALDBRÖL—THURSDAY

I have worked quite hard at my novel today. This morning we went to see the Ascension Day procession, and it rained like hell on the poor devils. Yesterday, when we were driving home, luckily in a closed carriage, the hail came on in immense stones, as big as walnuts, the largest. The place seemed covered with lumps of sugar.

You are far more ill than I am, now. Can't you begin to get well? It makes me miserable to think of you so badly off the hooks. No, I am well here. I am always well. But last week made me feel queer—in my soul mostly—and I want to get that well before I start the new enterprise of living with you. Does it seem strange to you? Give me till tomorrow or Saturday week, will you? I think it is better for us both. Till the twenty-fourth or twenty-fifth give me. Does it seem unloving and unnatural to you? No? See, when the airman fell, I was only a weak spot in your soul. Round the thought of me*—all your fear. Don't let it be so. Believe in me enough.*

Perhaps it is a bit of the monk in me. No, it is not. It is simply a desire to start with you, having a strong, healthy soul. The letters seem a long time getting from me to you. Tell me you understand, and you think it is—at least perhaps, *best. A good deal depends on the start. You never got over your bad beginning with E. . . .*

If you want H . . ., or anybody, have him. But I don't want anybody, till I see you. But all natures aren't alike. But I don't believe even you *are your best, when you are using H . . . as a dose of morphia—he's not much else to you. But sometimes one needs a dose of morphia, I've had many a one. So you know best. Only, my dear, because I love you, don't be sick, do will to be well and sane.*

This is also a long wait. I also am a carcass without you. But having a rather sick soul, I'll let it get up and be stronger before I ask it to run and live with you again.

Because, I'm not coming to you now *for rest, but to start living. It's a marriage, not a meeting. What an inevitable thing it seems. Only inevitable things—things that feel inevitable—are right. I am still a trifle afraid, but I know we are right. One is afraid to be born, I'm sure.*

I have written and written and written. I shall be glad to know you understand. I wonder if you'll be ill. Don't, if you can help it. But if you need *me—Frieda!*

Vale!

D. H. LAWRENCE

WALDBRÖL—FRIDAY

That was the letter I expected—and I hated it. Never mind. I suppose I deserve it all. I shall register it up, the number of times I leave you in the lurch: that is a historical phrase also. This is the first time. "Rats" is a bit hard, as a collective name for all your men—and you're the ship. Poor H . . ., poor devil! Vous le croquez bien entre les dents. I don't wonder E . . . hates your letters—they would drive any man on earth mad. I have not the faintest intention of dying: I hope you haven't any longer. I am not a tyrant. If I am, you will always have your own way. So my domain of tyranny isn't wide.—I am trying to think of some other mildly sarcastic things to say. Oh —the voice of Hannah, my dear, is the voice of a woman who laughs at her newly married husband when he's a bit tipsy and a big fool. You fling H . . . in my teeth. I shall say Hannah is getting fonder and fonder of me. She gives me *the best in the house. So there!*

I think I've exhausted my shell and shrapnel. You are getting better, thank the Lord. I am better quite. We have both, I think, marvellous recuperative powers.

You really seriously and honestly think I could come to Munich next Saturday, and stay two months, till August? You think we could manage it all right, as far as the business side goes? I begin to feel like rising once more on the wing. Ich komm —je viens—I come—advenio.

We are going to be married, respectable people, later on. If you were my property, I should have to look after you, which God forbid.

I like the way you stick to your guns. It's rather splendid. We won't fight, because you'd win, from sheer lack of sense of danger.

I think you're rather horrid to H. . . . You make him more babified—baby-fied. Or shall you leave him more manly?

You make me think of Maupassant's story. An Italian workman, a young man, was crossing in the train to France, and had no money, and had eaten nothing for a long time. There came a woman with breasts full of milk—she was going into France as a wet nurse. Her breasts full of milk hurt her—the young man was in a bad way with hunger. They relieved each other and went their several ways. Only where is H . . . to get his next feed?—Am I horrid?

Write to me quick from Munich, and I will tell them here. I can return here in August.

Be well, and happy, I charge you (tyranny)

D. H. Lawrence

GOING AWAY TOGETHER

I found these letters by accident in my mother's writing desk after Lawrence's death. At the time he wrote them, I was in such a bewildered state of mind, the depth of their feeling did not touch me, all I wanted was to be with him and have peace. I have not found my letters to him.

Isartal

LAST NIGHT I looked into the flames that leap in the big adobe fireplace that Lawrence built with the Indians, here at the ranch, in my room. He found an iron hoop to make the large curve of the fireplace. I don't know how he did it but the chimney draws well, the big logs burn fast.

Those leaping flames seemed he himself flickering in the night. This morning I found the wild red columbines that I had first found with him. There they were at my feet, in the hollow where the workmen have been cutting the logs for the new house. A delicate blaze of startling red and yellow, in front of me, the columbines, like gay small flags.

A rabbit stood still behind an oak shrub and watched me. A humming-bird hummed at me in consternation, as startled at me as I was at him. These things are Lawrence to me.

I shrink from remembering and putting down that almost too great intensity of our life together. I resent committing to paper for others to read what was so magic and new, our first being together. I wanted to keep it secret, all to myself, secretly I wanted to exult in the riches he gave me of himself and me and all the world.

But I owe it to him and to myself to write the truth as well as I can. I laugh at the claims of others that he might have loved them and that he didn't care for me at all. He cared only too much. I laugh when they write of him as a lonely genius dying alone. It is all my eye. The absolute, simple truth is so very simple.

I laugh when they want to make him out a brutal, ridiculous figure, he who was so tender and generous and fierce.

What does it amount to that he hit out at me in a rage, when I exasperated him, or mostly when the life around him drove him to the end of his patience? I didn't care very much. I hit back or waited till the storm in him subsided. We fought our battles outright to the bitter end. Then there was peace, such peace.

I preferred it that way. Battles must be. If he had sulked or borne me a grudge, how tedious!

What happened, happened out of the deep necessity of our natures. We were out for more than the obvious or "a little grey home in the West." Let them jeer at him, those superior people, it will not take away a scrap of his greatness or his genuineness or his love. To understand what happened between us, one must have had the experiences we had, thrown away as much as we did and gained as much, and have known this fulfilment of body and soul. It is not likely that many did.

'''

But here I am far from the little top floor in the Bavarian peasant-house in the Isartal.

Lawrence had met me in Munich.

He had given up the idea of a lectureship at a German University and from now on he lived by his writing. A new phase of life was beginning for both of us. But on me lay still heavily the children I had left behind and could not forget. But we were together, Lawrence and I. A friend had lent us the little top flat with its balcony, three rooms and a little kitchen.

The Alps floated above us in palest blue in the early morning. The Isar rushed its glacier waters and hurried the rafts along in the valley below. The great beechwoods stretched for hours behind us, to the Tegernsee.

Here we began our life together. And what a life! We had very little money, about fifteen shillings a week. We lived on black bread that Lawrence loved, fresh eggs, and "ripple"; later we found strawberries, raspberries, and "Heidelbeeren."

We had lost all ordinary sense of time and place. Those flowers that came new to Lawrence, the fireflies at night and the glow-worms, the first beech leaves spreading on the trees like a delicate veil overhead, and our feet buried in last year's brown beech leaves, these were our time and our events.

When Lawrence first found a gentian, a big single blue one, I remember feeling as if he had a strange communion with it, as if the gentian yielded up its blueness, its very essence, to him. Everything he met had the newness of a creation just that moment come into being.

I didn't want people, I didn't want anything, I only wanted to revel in this new world Lawrence had given me. I had found what I needed, I could now flourish like a trout in a stream or a daisy in the sun. His generosity in giving himself: "Take all you want of me, everything, I am yours"; and I took and gave equally, without thought.

When I asked him: "What do I give you, that you didn't get from others?" he answered: "You make me sure of myself, whole."

And he would say: "You are so young, so young!" When I remonstrated: "But I am older than you."—"Ah, it isn't years, it's something else. You don't understand."

Anyhow I knew he loved the essence of me as he loved the

blueness of the gentians, whatever faults I had. It was life to me.

"You have a genius for living," he told me.

"Maybe, but you brought it out in me."

But there were awful nights when he was still ill and feverish and delirious and I was frightened. Death seemed close. But the shadow of sickness soon vanished in the healthy, happy life we lived. He became strong, and full of energy and hope.

He would do nearly all the work of the small flat, bring the breakfast to me with a bunch of flowers that Frau Leitner had left on the milk jug in the early morning.

Frau Leitner had a shop underneath, with shoestrings and sweets, and bacon and brooms and everything under the sun. She gave Lawrence, whom she called "Herr Doktor," tastes of her "Heidelbeerschnapps," talking to him in her Bavarian dialect, while I, in a dream of wellbeing, would let time slip by. When I spilt coffee on the pillow I would only turn the pillow over. Nothing mattered except feeling myself live, and him. We talked and argued about everything. Vividly he would present to me all the people he had known in his youth, Walker Street with all its inhabitants, the close intimate life of what, for a better word, I called the common people; his mother, such a queen in her little house, and his father, down at the pit, sharing lunch with the pit-pony. It all seemed romantic to me. And the colliers being drunk on Friday nights and battles going on inevitably, it seemed, every Friday night in nearly all the houses, like a weekly hysteria. I listened enchanted by the hour. But poverty in his home was grievous. Lawrence would never have been so desperately ill if his mother could have given him all the care he needed and the food she could not afford to buy for him with the little money she had.

Bitter it was to him when a friend at the high school who took him home to tea, refused to continue the friendship as soon as he heard Lawrence was a miner's son. Then I would tell him about my early life in Lorraine. Mine had been a happy childhood. We had a lovely house and gardens outside Metz. I lived through the flowers, as they came: snowdrops, scyllae and crocuses, the enormous oriental poppies in their vivid green leaves so overwhelmingly near one's small face, the delicate male irises. My father would pick the first asparagus and I would trot behind his bent back. Later in the summer I lived on the fruit trees: cherry, pear, apple, plum, peach trees. I would even go to sleep on them and fall off, sometimes, trying to do my lessons up in them. I did not like school.

First I went to a convent, where I did not learn very much. "Toujours doucement, ma petite Frieda," they would say to me as I came dashing into class with my Hessian boots. But it was no use; I was a wild child and they could not tame me, those gentle nuns. I was happiest with the soldiers, who had temporary barracks outside our house for years. They invited my sister Johanna and me to their big Christmas tree hung with sausages, cigars, "hearts of gingerbread," packages from home, and little dolls they had carved for us. And they sang for us accompanied by their mournful harmonicas:

"*Wenn ich zu meinem Kinde geh.*"

Once my father's old regiment acted the occasion on which he had received his iron cross in the Franco-Prussian War. It was on the Kaiser's birthday. After the ceremony the soldiers lifted my father on their shoulders and carried him through the hall. My heart beat to bursting: "What a hero my father is!"

But a few days after one of my special friends, a corporal, told me how he hated being a soldier, how bullied you were, how unjust and stupid it all was, that military life. He stood there talking to me in the garden path, in his bright blue uniform, while he tied some roses. He had a mark over his bed for each day he had still to serve, he told me. A hundred and nineteen more there were, he said. I looked up at him and understood his suffering. After that the flags of the dragoons and the splendid bands of the regiments had no longer the same glamour as they passed along the end of the garden to the Exerzierplatz.

When the regiments were filing past, Johanna and I sat on the garden wall, very grandly. Then we would throw pears and apples into the ranks. Great confusion would arise. An irate major turned toward his men and yelled, we popped quickly out of sight behind the wall, only to reappear and begin anew.

What I loved most of all was playing with my boy friends in the fortifications around Metz, among the huts and trenches the soldiers had built. I always liked being with boys and men. Only they gave me the kind of interest I wanted. Women and girls frightened me. My adolescence and youth puzzled me. Pleasure and social stuff left me unsatisfied. There was something more I wanted, I wanted so much. Where would I get it, and from whom? With Lawrence I found what I wanted. All the exuberance of my childhood came back to me.

"'

One day I bathed in the Isar and a heel came off one of my shoes on the rough shore; so I took both shoes off and threw them into the Isar. Lawrence looked at me in amazement. "He's shocked, as I must walk home barefoot, but it's a lonely road, it doesn't matter," I thought. But it wasn't that; he was shocked at my wastefulness.

He lectured me: "A pair of shoes takes a long time to make and you should respect the labour somebody's put into those shoes."

To which I answered: "Things are there for me and not I for them, so when they are a nuisance I throw them away."

I was very untidy and careless, so he took great pains to make me more orderly. "Look, put your woollen things in this drawer, in this one your silk clothes, and here your cotton ones."

It sounded amusing, so I did it.

When I said: "But I like to be like the lilies in the field, who do not spin."

"What! Don't they just work hard, those lilies," was his reply. "They have to bring up their sap, produce their leaves, flowers and seeds!" That was that. Later on he aroused my self-respect. "You can't even make a decent cup of coffee. Any common woman can do lots of things that you can't do."

"Oh," I thought, "I'll show him if I can't." But that was later on.

One day, in Munich, seeing all the elegant people in the streets I had an aristocratic fit. I bought some handkerchiefs with an *F* and a little crown on them. When I brought them home he said: "Now I'll draw *my* coat-of-arms." He drew a pickaxe, a school-board, a fountain pen with two lions rampant. "When they make me a Lord, which they never will," he said. Then, half jokingly, but I took it seriously: "Would you like me to become King of England?" I was distressed. "Isn't he satisfied, the whole universe is ours, does he want to be so dull a thing as a king?" But I never doubted that he might have been a king if he wanted to. Then he would write poems for me, poems I took a little anxiously, seeing he knew me so well.

He would go for walks by himself, and his quick, light feet coming home told me in their footfall how he had enjoyed his adventure.

He would have a large, heroic bunch of flowers, or a tight little posy for me or a bright bird's feather.

Then the story of his adventure, a deer peeping at him inquisitively from the underbrush, a handsome Bavarian peasant he had spoken to, how raspberries were just coming out, soldiers marching along the road.

Then again we would be thrown out of our paradisial state. Letters would come. The harm we had done; my grief for my children would return red hot.

But Lawrence would console me and say: "Don't be sad, I'll make a new heaven and earth for them, don't cry, you see if I don't." I would be consoled yet he was furious when I went on. "You don't care a damn about those brats really, and they don't care about you." I cried and we quarrelled.

"What kind of an unnatural woman would I be if I could forget my children?" Yet my agony over them was my worst crime in his eyes. He seemed to make that agony more acute in me than it need have been. Perhaps he, who had loved his mother so much, felt, somewhere, it was almost impossible for a mother to leave her children. But I was so sure: "This bond is for ever, nothing in heaven or earth can break it. I must wait, I must wait!"

My father had written: "You travel about the world like a

barmaid." It was a grief to him, who loved me, that I was so poor, and socially impossible.

I only felt wonderfully free, "vogelfrei" indeed. To Lawrence fell the brunt of the fight, and he protected me. "You don't know how I stand between you and the world," he said, later on. If I supported him with all my might, the wings of his sure spirit made a shelter for me always.

111

Now I lie writing by the stream, where it makes a little pool. The bushes all around form an enclosed shelter for bathing, while in front stretches the alfalfa field, then the trees, then the desert, so vast and changing with sun and shadow. Curtains of rain, floating clouds, grey, delicate, thin but to the west today white, large, round, billowing.

It is the end of June. I wonder if the strawberries are ripe, in the hollow by the aqueduct, or if the wild roses are out, the very pink ones, along the stream by the Gallina. Shall I see a wild turkey, if I walk along the path Lawrence took so often, I running behind, to the mouth of the Gallina?

He and Mr. Murry laid the big pipes on pillars of wood to bring the water along. Where tall aspens stand and the Gallina waters come tearing down. Often the pipes had to be fixed, after a cloudburst had broken the whole thing down.

Here at the ranch we are alive and busy, but Lawrence will see it no more.

Last night the coyotes have torn to pieces a young sheep, on the ranch. Poor thing, that looked at me with scared sheep's eyes, when I drew near. How hateful coyotes are. Mr. Murry tells me they even play with lambs, whisking their tails among them, to get them away more easily. Nature sweet and pure!

This is one of the perfect moments here. The days are

swinging their serene hours across the immense skies, the sun sets splendidly, then a star comes, and the young moon in the old moon's arms. The water sings louder than in the daytime. More and more stars come as the light fades out of the western sky.

But then, in the silence of the beautiful night, the coyotes, a few yards from the house, tore the lamb to pieces. How I wish someone would shoot them all, but they are hard to shoot.

⸙⸙⸙

Here I am in the present again, when I want to write of the past. I will go back to Icking, our village in the Isartal, and that young Lawrence who was beginning to spread his wings.

I think of my going into a chapel, in a village near Beuerberg. I looked at the Madonna on the altar; she wasn't a *mater dolorosa*, nor of the spiritual sort, she was of the placid peasant type, and I said to her: "Yes, you have a halo round your head, but I feel as if I had a halo around the whole of me, that's how *he* makes me feel. You have nothing but a dead son. It doesn't seem good enough for me. Give me a live man."

Sitting on a little landing pier, once, by the Kochelsee, dangling our feet in the clear water of the lake, Lawrence was putting the rings of my fingers on my toes to see how they looked in the clear water. Suddenly a shower overtook us. There was a bunch of trees behind, and a road going in both directions. We ran for shelter and must have run in opposite ways. I looked all around but Lawrence was not there. A great fear came over me. I had lost him, perhaps he was drowned, slipped into the lake. I called, I went to look, somehow he had dissolved into the air. I should never see him

LAWRENCE [THE SMALLEST OF THE BOYS]
AND HIS FAMILY

again. There was always this "not of the earth" quality about him.

By the time I saw him coming down the road, an hour later, I was almost in hysterics. "Brother Moonshine" I called him, as in the German fairytale. He didn't like that.

Then he would sit in a corner, so quietly and absorbedly, to write. The words seemed to pour out of his hand onto the paper, unconsciously, naturally and without effort, as flowers bloom and birds fly past.

His was a strange concentration, he seemed transferred into another world, the world of creation.

He'd have quick changes of mood and thought. This puzzled me. "But Lawrence, last week you said exactly the opposite of what you are saying now."

"And why shouldn't I? Last week I felt like that, now like this. Why shouldn't I?"

We talked about style in writing, about the new style Americans had evolved—cinematographic, he called it.

All this idea of style and form puzzled Lawrence.

For my part, I felt certain that a genuine creation would take its own form inevitably, the way every living thing does.

All those phrases "Art for art's sake," "Le style c'est l'homme," are all very well but they aren't creation. But Lawrence had to be quite sure in everything.

On some evenings he would be so gay and act a whole revival meeting for me, as in the chapel of his home town.

There was the revivalist parson. He would work his congregation up to a frenzy; then, licking his finger to turn the imaginary pages of the book of Judgment and suddenly darting a finger at some sinner in the congregation: "Is *your* name written in the book?" he would shout.

A collier's wife in a little sailor straw hat, in a frenzy of repentance, would clatter down the aisle, throw herself on her knees in front of the altar, and pray: "O Lord, our Henry, he would 'ave come too, only he dursn't, O Lord, so I come as well for him, O Lord!" It was a marvellous scene! First as the parson then as the collier's wife Lawrence made me shake with laughter. He told me how desperately ill he had been at sixteen, with inflammation of the lungs, how he was almost dead but fought his way back to life with the fierce courage and vitality that was his. It made me long to make him strong and healthy.

Healthy in soul he always was. He may have been cross and irritable sometimes but he was never sorry for himself and all he suffered.

This poem was written in the Isartal:

SONG OF A MAN WHO IS LOVED

Between her breasts is my home, between her breasts.
Three sides set on me space and fear, but the fourth side rests,
Warm in a city of strength, between her breasts.

All day long I am busy and happy at my work
I need not glance over my shoulder in fear of the terrors that lurk
Behind. I am fortified, I am glad at my work.

I need not look after my soul; beguile my fear
With prayer, I need only come home each night to find the dear
Door on the latch, and shut myself in, shut out fear.

I need only come home each night and lay
My face between her breasts;
And what of good I have given the day, my peace attests.

And what I have failed in, what I have wronged
Comes up unnamed from her body and surely
Silent tongued I am ashamed.

And I hope to spend eternity
With my face down-buried between her breasts
And my still heart full of security
And my still hands full of her breasts.

FRIEDA IN BAVARIAN COSTUME

Walking to Italy

It is five o'clock in the morning. The air is fresh after last night's heavy rain. There is a slight mist, but the sun from the desert is driving it away.

Suddenly it comes over me so strongly that Lawrence is dead, really dead. The grief for his loss will be my steady companion for the rest of my life. Sometimes it will be a friend, consoling me, putting everything in proper proportion. And sometimes this grief will follow me, dogging my footsteps like a hyena, not wanting me to live. Never will anything matter so desperately any more.

I remember Lawrence saying to me: "You always identify yourself with life, why do you?"

I answered: "Because I feel like it."

I know now how completely he trusted his life to me, he in whom death was always so near.

I hated that death and I fought against it like a demon, unconsciously on my own. I did not know he was consumptive till years later when the doctor in Mexico told me. All my life with him there was this secret fear that I could not share with him. I had to bear it alone. Then in the end I knew, and it was an awful knowledge, that I could do no more. Death was stronger than I. His life hung by a thread and one day that thread would break. He would die before his time.

This true mountain morning takes me back to our journey across the Alps.

It was in the middle of August that we set out gaily. Neither of us knew Italy at the time, it was a great adventure for both. We packed up our few possessions, three trunks went ahead of us to the Lago di Garda. We set off on foot, with a rucksack each and a Burberry. In the rucksack was a little spirit lamp, we were going to cook our food by the roadside for cheapness.

We started on a misty morning very thrilled. The trees were dripping along the road, but we were happy in our adventure, free, going to unknown parts. We walked along the solid green of the valley of the Isar, we climbed up hills and went down again. One of my desires, to sleep in haylofts, was fulfilled. But sleeping in haylofts is uncomfortable, really. It rained so much and we were soaked. And the wind blows through haylofts and if you cover yourself with a ton of hay you still can't get warm. Lawrence has described the crucifixes we passed, the lovely chapel he found high up in the mountains. He lit the candles on the altar, for it was evening, read all the ex-votos and forgot how tired and hungry he was.

Here are some poems he wrote about this time:

ALL OF ROSES

I

By the Isar, in the twilight
We were wandering and singing:
By the Isar, in the evening
We climbed the huntsman's ladder and sat swinging
In the fir-tree overlooking the marshes;
While river met river, and the ringing
Of their pale-green glacier-water filled the evening.

By the Isar, in the twilight
We found our warm wild roses
Hanging red at the river; and simmering
Frogs were singing, and over the river closes
Was scent of roses, and glimmering
In the twilight, our kisses across the roses
Met, and her face, and my face, were roses.

II

When she rises in the morning
I linger to watch her.
She stands in silhouette against the window
And the sunbeams catch her
Glistening white on the shoulders:
        While down her sides, the mellow
        Golden shadow glows, and her breasts
        Swing like full-blown yellow
        Gloire de Dijon roses.

She drips herself with water
And her shoulders
Glisten as silver, they crumple up
Like wet and shaken roses, and I listen
For the rustling of their white, unfolding petals.
In the window full of sunlight
She stirs her golden shadow
And flashes all herself as sunbright
As if roses fought with roses.

III

Just a few of the roses we gathered from the Isar
Are fallen, and their mauve-red petals on the cloth
Float like boats on a river, waiting
For a fairy-wind to wake them from their sloth.

She laughs at me across the table, saying
She loves me, and I blow a little boat
Rocking down the shoals between the tea-cups
And so kiss-beladen that it scarce can float.

IV

Slow like a rose comes tip-toe out of bud
I see the woman's soul steal in her eyes,
And wide in ecstasy I sit and watch
The unknown flower issued magic-wise.

And day by day out of the envious bud
My treasure softly slips uncurled,
And day by day my happiness vibrates
In wide and wider circles round the world.

Lawrence's birthday came as we were crossing the Alps. I had no present to give him but some edelweiss. That evening we danced and drank beer with the peasants in the Gasthaus of the village we were passing through. His first birthday together. It was all very wonderful. New things happened all the time.

Here is a poem Lawrence wrote:

MEETING AMONG THE MOUNTAINS

The little pansies by the road have turned
Away their purple faces and their gold;
And evening has taken all the bees from the wild thyme
And all the scent is shed away by the cold.

Against the hard pale-blue evening sky
The mountains' new-dropped summer snow is clear
Glistening in steadfast stillness—clear
Like clean pain sending on us a chill down here.

Christ on the cross, his beautiful young man's body
Has fallen forward on the nails, and hangs
White and loose at last, with all his pain
Drawn on his mouth, eyes broken in the final pangs.

And slowly down the mountain road, a belated
Bullock waggon comes: Lo I am ashamed
To gaze any more at the Christ, whom the mountain snows
Whitely confront, my heart shrinks back, inflamed.

The breath of the bullock steams on the hard chill air;
The band across its brow, it scarcely seems
To draw the load, so slow and dull it moves
While the driver sits on the left-hand shaft and dreams.

Surely among your sunbrowned hand, some face, something
That vexes me with memory! He sits so still
Here among all this silence, crouching forwara
Dreaming and letting the bullock take its will.

I stand aside on the grass to let them go,
And, Christ, again have I met his eyes, again
The brown eyes black with misery and hate, that look
Full into mine, and the torment starts again.

One moment the hate leaps at me standing there,
One moment I see the stillness of agony
Something frozen in silence, that dare not be
Loosed; one moment the darkness frightens me.

Then among the averted pansies, below the high
White peaks of snow, at the foot of the sunken Christ,
I stood in a chill of anguish, trying to say
The joy I bought was not too highly priced.

But he was gone, motionless, hating me,
Enduring as the mountains do, because they are strong
But a pale dead Christ on the crucifix of his heart
And breathing the frozen memory of his wrong.

Still in his nostrils the frozen breath of despair,
And in his heart the half-numbed agony;
In his clenched fist the shame and in
His belly the smouldering hate of me.

And I, as I stand in the cold averted flowers,
Feel the shame that clenches his fists like nails through my own,
Feel the despair on his brow like a crown of thorns
And his frozen anguish turning my heart to stone.

TUXTAL

How I want to recapture the gaiety of that adventurous walk into Italy, romantic Italy, with all its glamour and sunshine.

We arrived at Trento, but alas for the glamour! We could only afford a very cheap hotel and the marks on the walls, the doubtful sheets, and worst of all the W.C.'s were too much for me.

The people were strangers, I could not speak Italian, then.

So, one morning, much to Lawrence's dismay, he found me sitting on a bench under the statue of Dante, weeping bitterly. He had seen me walk barefoot over icy stubble, laughing at wet and hunger and cold; it had all seemed only fun to me, and here I was crying because of the city-uncleanness and the W.C.'s. It had taken us about six weeks to get there.

We took the train to Riva on the Lago di Garda. It was an Austrian garrison town at that time. Elegant officers in biscuit-coloured trousers and pale-blue jackets walked about with equally elegant ladies. For the first time I looked at Lawrence and myself; two tramps with rucksacks! Lawrence's trousers were frayed, Miriam's trousers we called them, for he had bought them with "Miriam." I had a reddish cotton crêpe dress all uneven waves at the skirt; the colour of the red velvet ribbon had run into my panama hat. I was grateful to the three ladies who took us into their pensione and, instead of fearing the worst for their silver, sent us yellow and blue figs and grapes to our room, where we cooked our meals on the spirit lamp for economy, in fear and trembling of the housemaid. Then we got our trunks.

My sister Johanna had sent me lovely clothes and hats, some "Paquins," much too elegant for our circumstances; but we dressed up proudly and set forth in triumph.

At Gargnano we found Villa Igea to spend the winter.

Lawrence for the first time had a place of his own. The first floor of a large villa, our windows looking over the lake, the road running underneath, opposite us the Monte Baldo in rosy sunsets. "Green star Sirius dribbling over the lake," as Lawrence says in one of his poems.

Here began my first attempt at housekeeping. It was uphill work, in that big bare kitchen with the "fornelli" and the big copper pans. Often the stews and "fritti" had to be rescued, and he would come nobly from his work, never grumbling, when I called: "Lorenzo, the pigeons are burning, what shall I do?"

The first time I washed sheets was a disaster. They were so large and wet, their wetness was overwhelming. The kitchen floor was flooded, the table drenched, I dripped from hair to feet.

When Lawrence found me all misery he called: "The One and Only" (which name stood for the one and only phœnix, when I was uppish) "is drowning, oh, dear!" I was rescued and dried, the kitchen wiped and soon the sheets were hanging to dry in the garden where the "cachi" were hanging red from the trees. One morning he brought me breakfast in bed and in the Italian bedroom there was a spittoon and to my horror a scorpion was on it. To Lawrence's surprise I said, when he killed it: "Birds of a feather flock together."

"Ungrateful woman . . . here I am the faithful knight killing the dragons and that's all I get."

One of our favourite walks was to Bogliacco, the next village on the Garda, where we drank wine and ate chestnuts with the Bersaglieri who seemed quiet and sad and didn't say much. My window high up over the road was a joy to me.

Bersaglieri came past in their running march with a gay spark of a tenente at their head, singing: "Tripoli sara' Italiana." Secretly people did their bargaining under my windows, at night the youths played their guitars; when I peeped Lawrence was cross.

He was then rewriting his "Sons and Lovers," the first book he wrote with me, and I lived and suffered that book, and wrote bits of it when he would ask me: "What do you think my mother felt like then?" I had to go deeply into the character of Miriam and all the others; when he wrote his mother's death he was ill and his grief made me ill too, and he said: "If my mother had lived I could never have loved you, she wouldn't have let me go." But I think he got over it; only, this fierce and overpowerful love had harmed the boy who was not strong enough to bear it. In after years he said: "I would write a different 'Sons and Lovers' now; my mother was wrong, and I thought she was absolutely right."

I think a man is born twice: first his mother bears him, then he has to be reborn from the woman he loves. Once, sitting on the little steamer on the lake he said: "Look, that little woman is like my mother." His mother, though dead, seemed so alive and *there* still to him.

Towards the end of "Sons and Lovers" I got fed up and turned against all this "house of Atreus" feeling, and I wrote a skit called: "Paul Morel, or His Mother's Darling." He read it and said, coldly: "This kind of thing isn't called a skit."

While we were at Villa Igea Lawrence wrote also "Twilight in Italy," and most of the poems from "Look! We Have Come Through!"

His courage in facing the dark recesses of his own soul impressed me always, scared me sometimes.

In his heart of hearts I think he always dreaded women, felt that they were in the end more powerful than men. Woman is so absolute and undeniable. Man moves, his spirit flies here and there, but you can't go beyond a woman. From her man is born and to her he returns for his ultimate need of body and soul. She is like earth and death to which all return.

Here is a poem:

THE MOTHER OF SONS

This is the last of all, then, this is the last!
I must fold my hands, and turn my face to the fire,
And watch my dead days fusing into dross,
Shape after shape, and scene after scene, from the past
Sinking to one dead mass in the dying fire
Leaving the grey ash cold and heavy with loss.

Strange he is to me, my son, whom I waited like a lover;
Strange as the captive held in a foreign country, haunting
The shore and gazing out on the level sea;
White, and gaunt, with wistful eyes that hover
Always upon the distance, as his soul was chaunting
The dreary weird of departure from me.

Like a young bird blown from out of the frozen seas,
Like a bird from the far north blown with a broken wing
Into our sooty garden, he drags and beats
From place to place perpetually, and seeks release
From me, and the hound of my love that creeps up fawning
For his mastership, while he in displeasure retreats.

I must look away from him, for my fading eyes
Like a cringing dog at his heels offend him now,
Like a toothless hound pursuing him with my eyes,
Till he chafes at my cringing persistence, and a sharp spark flies
Into my soul from the sudden fall of his brow
And he bites his lip in pain as he hears my sighs.

WALKING TO ITALY

This is the last—it will not be any more—
All my life I have borne the burden of myself,
All the long years of sitting in my husband's house,
And never have I said to myself, as he closed the door:
"Now I am caught.—You are hopelessly lost, O self,
You are frightened with joy, my heart, like a frightenea mouse."

Three times have I offered my soul—three times rejected—
It will not be any more—no more, my son, my son!
Never to know the glad freedom of obedience, since long ago
The angel of childhood kissed me and went.—I expected
A man would take me, and now, my son, oh my son
I must sit awhile and wait and never know
A bridegroom, till 'twixt me and the bright sun

Death, in whose service is nothing of gladness, takes me.
—For the lips and the eyes of God are behind a veil,
And the thought of the lipless voice of the Father shakes me
With fear and fills my eyes with tears of desire,
But the voice of my life is dumb and of no avail,
And the hands in my lap grow cold as the night draws nigher.

And always again the mail and tragedy. I was so sure I would be able to be with my children but finally my husband wrote: "If you don't come home the children have no longer any mother, you shall not see them again." I was almost beside myself with grief. But Lawrence held me, I could not leave him any more, he needed me more than they did.

But I was like a cat without her kittens, and always in my mind was the care, "Now if they came where would I put them to sleep?" I felt the separation physically as if something tore at my navel-string. And Lawrence could not bear it, it was too much for him. And then again I would turn to him and be healed and forget for a while.

Everybody seemed to condemn us and be against us and I couldn't for the life of me understand how the whole world couldn't see how right and wonderful it was to live as we did; I just couldn't. I said: "Lorenzo, why can't people live as happily and get as much out of life as we do? Everybody could, with the little money we spend." And he answered: "You forget that I'm a genius," half in fun and half seriously.

I wasn't impressed by the genius at that time, making a long nose at him, taking everything like the wind and the rain, but now I know that the glamour of it all was his genius.

He was always absolutely sure of himself, sure that the Lord was with him. Once we had a big storm on our way to Australia and I said, afraid: "Now, if this ship goes down . . ." He answered: "The ship that I am on won't go down."

Here follow some letters he wrote to my sister Else:

VILLA IGEA
VILLA DI GARGNANO
LAGO DI GARDA
14 DEC. 1912

Dear Else:

I was not cross with your letter. I think you want to do the best for Frieda. I do also. But I think you ask us to throw away a real apple for a gilt one. Nowadays it costs more courage to assert one's desire and need, than it does to renounce. If Frieda and the children could live happily together, I should say "Go" because the happiness of two out of three is sufficient. But if she would only be sacrificing her life, I would not let her go if I could keep her. Because if she brings to the children a sacrifice, that is a curse to them. If I had a prayer, I think it would be "Lord, let no one ever sacrifice living stuff to me—because I am burdened enough."

Whatever the children may miss now, they will preserve their inner liberty, and their independent pride will be strong when they come of age. But if Frieda gave all up to go and live with them, that would sap their strength because they would have to support her life when they grew up. They would not be free to live of themselves—they would first have to live for her, *to pay back. It is like somebody giving a present that was never asked for, and putting the recipient under the obligation of making restitution, often more than he could afford.*

So we must go on, and never let go the children, but will, will and will to have them and have what we think good. That's all one can do. You say: "Lawrence kommt mir vor wie ein

Held"—I hope he may "gehen dir aus" similarly. He doesn't feel at all heroic, but only in the devil of a mess.

Don't mind how I write, will you?

Yours sincerely,

D. H. Lawrence

Villa Igea
Villa di Gargnano
Lago di Garda (Brescia)
10 Feb. 1913

Dear Else:

You don't expect me to stay here, gaping like a fish out of water, while Frieda goes careering and carousing off to München, do you? Je vous en veux.

About the article—Frieda is a nameless duffer at telling anything—the English Review*—a shilling monthly, supposed to be advanced and clever—asked me to write an article on modern German poetry—about three thousand words. It is the modern, new stuff they want to hear about—say that which is published in the last ten years—such people as Dehmel, and Liliencron, Stefan George, Ricarda Huch, Elsa Laska Schule. Haven't you got a strong opinion about modern German poetry—pottery, as father calls it? Well, do write about what you think—say Dehmel is ranty and tawdry, if you like, but don't be too classical. If you like, the* English Review *will listen with great respect to dithyrambs on beautiful printing and fine form in book issuing.*

It will adore tendency, and influences. And for heaven's sake, put in plenty of little poems or verses as examples.—It would be rather a cute idea to write about: "The Woman-Poets of the Germany of Today" or "The Woman-Poets of Germany Today."

It would fetch the English Review *readers like pigeons to salt. And surely* Die Frau *has got articles on the subject. I should love doing it myself if I knew enough about it. (Nicht wahr—I have reviewed, in England, two anthologies of modern German Poetry.)*

Do write about the women—their aims and ideals—and a bit about them personally, any you know and how they'd rather paint pictures than nurse children, because any motherly body can do the latter, while it needs a fine and wonderful woman to speak a message. Didn't somebody tell you that? Did she have red hair? Put it all in.

"The Woman-Poets of Germany Today," it sounds lovely. Do write it in German—I can read your letters quite easily, because you don't write in Gothic hieroglyphs.

It is beautiful weather here. We are finding the first violets. There are bunches of primroses everywhere, and Leber Blumen, lovely little blue things, and lilac-coloured crocuses. You must come, you would love it, and we should feel quite grand having you for a visitor.

Mrs. K . . . has written, forwarding a lawyer's letter which was sent to E . . . , and which says: "We should advise Professor W . . . to refer Mrs. W . . . to the Court, pending the divorce proceedings. Any request she had to make concerning the children, should be made to the Court." That of course necessitates the engaging of a solicitor.

Frieda says, it is too long to let the children wait another six months without seeing her—they would become too much estranged. Perhaps that is true. Heaven knows how we are going to untangle these knots. At any rate the divorce is going forward; in England, after the first hearing, the judge pronounces a decree nisi—*that is, the divorce is granted* unless *something turns up; then at the end of the six months the divorce is made* absolute, *if nothing has turned up. Then Frieda is free again. Till the divorce is absolute, E . . . must have nothing to do with Frieda. So arrangements should be made through lawyers. But the children have holidays only at Easter, and can anything be settled before then? We shall have to see. This is to put you au courant. Send that* wonderful *book, do. The sixty francs have come.*

Frieda is sending a picture that I want to have framed for Prof. Weber at Icking, but she says it is for you. And a thousand thanks.

D. H. Lawrence

1913-1914

In the spring I went from the Villa Igea to Baden-Baden and saw my father for the last time; he was ill and broken. "I don't understand the world any more," he said.

Lawrence walked over the big St. Bernard with a friend. We met in London after a fortnight to see my children and to arrange about the divorce. We stayed with the Garnetts. One morning I met my children on their way to their school. They danced around me in complete delight. "Mama, you are back, when are you coming home?"

"I can't come back, you must come to me. We shall have to wait."

How I suffered not to be able to take them with me! So much of my spontaneous living had gone to them and now this was cut off. When I tried to meet them another morning they had evidently been told that they must not speak to me and only little white faces looked at me as if I were an evil ghost. It was hard to bear, and Lawrence, in his helplessness, was in a rage.

We met Katherine Mansfield and Middleton Murry at that time. I think theirs was the only spontaneous and jolly friendship that we had. We had tea with Katherine in her flat in London. If I remember rightly her room had only cushions and pouffes and a large aquarium with goldfish and shells and plants.

I thought her so exquisite and complete, with her fine

brown hair, delicate skin, and brown eyes which we later called her "gu-gu" eyes. She was a perfect friend and tried her best to help me with the children. She went to see them, talked to them and took them letters from me. I loved her like a younger sister.

I fell for Katherine and Murry when I saw them quite unexpectedly on the top of a bus, making faces at each other and putting their tongues out.

We also met Cynthia and Herbert Asquith, at Margate. Cynthia seemed to me lovely as Botticelli's Venus. We also saw Eddie Marsh and Sir Walter Raleigh and Cynthia's relations at her house, which was an unusual one, made all of ship's timber. Cynthia was always a loyal friend, even through the war, when friends were rare.

But Lawrence wanted to go away from England, also bacause the divorce was not finished. Later we returned to Bavaria. There Lawrence wrote "The Prussian Officer." The strange struggle of those two opposite natures, the officer and his servant, seems to me particularly significant for Lawrence. He wrote it before the war but as if he had sensed it. The unhappy, conscious man, the superior in authority envying the other man his simple, satisfied nature. I felt as if he himself was both these people.

They seemed to represent the split in his soul, the split between the conscious and the unconscious man.

To grow into a complete whole out of the different elements that we are composed of is one of our most elemental tasks. It is a queer story and it frightened me at the time of the dark corners of Lawrence's soul, the human soul altogether. But his courage in facing the problems and horrors of life always impressed me. Often he was ill when his consciousness tried to penetrate into deeper strata, it was an interplay of body and soul and I in real agony would try to understand what was happening. He demanded so much of me and I *had* to be there for him so completely. Sometimes it was I who forced him to go deeper and roused his inner conflict. When I went away it was always terrible. He hated me for going away. "You use me as a scientist his 'dissecting rabbit,' I am your 'Versuchs Kaninchen,' " I told him.

✓✓✓

We wanted to go to Italy again.

The next winter we found a little cottage, "Fiascherino," near Lerici—finding a new more southern Italy and settling down for a while like gipsies in their camp; always more adventure.

We had a large piece of land with olive trees and vegetables running down to the little bay where we bathed and kept a flat-bottomed boat, on which Lawrence went out to sea through the surf. I was on the shore watching him like a hen who has hatched a duckling and yelled in a rage: "If you can't be a real poet, you'll drown like one, anyhow."

Shelley was drowned not so far away. I spent lazy days lying in a hammock watching the fishermen with their beautiful red-sailed boats underneath my high rock. I watched the submarines from Spezia bobbing up and down. We had a maid, Elide, who looked after us and loved us, and her mother Felice was mostly there too. "Bocca di mosca!" she would shout at her daughter. They loved us quite ferociously; fought to buy things cheaply for us in the market and felt absolutely responsible for us. One of Elide's griefs was that Lawrence would go out in his old clothes; she would rush after him with another coat: "Signor Lorenzo, Signor Lorenzo," and force him to put it on, which is more than I could have done. . . . When I took her along to Spezia for Christmas shopping she behaved as if she were attending the Queen of Italy at least, much to my chagrin. Nothing was too good for "la mia Signora. . . ."

We went once to visit the Waterfields at their lovely old castle, "Aula," near Sarzana. We slept there in such a terrifically large room that it overwhelmed us, the beds looked so tiny in the vast room that we brought them close together, to make a larger spot in the vastness . . . it was a beautiful place, high up above the Magra, wide river arms underneath . . . there were flowers growing on the wide fortress walls, a dantesque sunrise; we were impressed.

The cottage at Fiascherino had only three small rooms and a kitchen and I tried to make it look as cheerful as possible; it did not matter what I did with them, for we were out of doors most of the day; had our meals outdoors and took long walks, returning only when it grew dark, and built a fire in the downstairs room. I believe the chief tie between Lawrence and me was always the wonder of living . . . every little or big thing that happened carried its glamour with it.

But we also had sordid blows. Mitchell Kennerley of New York had bought copies of "Sons and Lovers" from Duckworth for America and sent a cheque for £25. As I had no money of my own, Lawrence said: "You can spend that for yourself." I took the cheque to the bank at La Spezia where they told me the date was altered, the cheque must go back to New York. It never returned. For "Sons and Lovers" Lawrence never got any money from America for about twelve years. Meanness made Lawrence always silently angry—it was something not to be thought of, but dismissed, nothing to be done, why waste your energy, then. But I, like a fool, talked furiously when I'd been disappointed. We had many such disappointments later on. With the dangerous quality of his work he accepted his more than doubtful financial position and I think one of my merits in his eyes was my never being eager to be rich or to play a role in the social world. It was hardly merit on my part, I enjoyed being poor and I didn't want to play a role in the world.

We had met many people who had villas round the bay of La Spezia, English and American. They were friendly, but I said to Lawrence: "I don't want to be a fraud, let's tell them that we aren't married; perhaps they won't like us any more if they know how it is."

One charming Miss Huntingdon, who had become a Catholic, was much distressed. "I am fond of you both," she wrote, "and far be it from me to judge you, but I must tell you that I believe you are wrong, your life together is a mistake, a sin." Her deep distress made me feel sorry for her, as if she had had to face the same problem and had chosen otherwise. But I was aware of the joyful acceptance and hope in me, that for my part I had chosen what was right. I don't understand, to this day, what social values really are and what meaning has the whole social game; social standards were never real to me, and the game didn't ever seem worth the candle. That winter in Fiascherino was a very happy one. He wrote "The Rainbow" there, "The Sisters" it was called at first. When Edward Garnett read it he didn't like it. This upset Lawrence, that Garnett did not follow his trend. But I said: "You are fighting the old standards, and breaking new ground." They said I ruined Lawrence's genius, but I know it is not so.

Lawrence was always busy, he taught me many songs, we

sang by the hour in the evenings; he liked my strong voice. He sang with very little voice but, like a real artist that he was, he conveyed the music and the spirit of the song in a marvellous fashion.

We painted together, too. I can see him so absorbed and intent, licking the brush, putting it down on the paper with quick gestures, giving himself completely to everything he was doing and not understanding that I did it all so carelessly and for fun.

I remember the day the piano arrived from Spezia by sea in a little boat and we watched it bobbing round the corner of the foreland, with three Italians, very frightened, fearing to go to the bottom of the sea with it. We felt for them, for it really looked very dangerous. Then at last they pulled up on the shingly beach and it was brought up to our little cottage with terrific shouts of "Avanti, Italiani!"

Christmas came and we had Elide's relations, about a dozen peasants, in the evening and they sang to us, very much at home with us. Elide's old mother, Felice, sang: "Da quella parte dove si lev il sol," and "Di' a la Marcella che lui sa far l'amor," with old Pasquale, a duet. The beautiful Luigi was there, who looked so handsome picking olives from the trees; also the Maestro from Telaro, who was in love with Luigi; but she was of higher station and he, alas, wasn't in love with her. I don't know if they ever were married or not. But always the tragedy came up . . . it got me from time to time like an illness. We had trespassed the laws of men, if not of God, and you have to pay. Lawrence and I paid in full, and the others, on the contrary, had to pay for *want* of love and tenderness, and nobody likes to pay. Yet it's an eternal human law: too much happiness isn't allowed us mere mortals. And

I and Lawrence seemed at times to surpass the measure of human bliss. He could be so deeply and richly happy, that young Lawrence that I have known, before the war crushed so much of his belief in human civilization. . . . His deep, natural love for his fellowmen. . . . The deadness of them, the mechanicalness that triumphed in their souls.

I asked: "What is civilization? What is it, this man-made world that I don't understand?"

And he said: "It's like a tree that comes forth out of a race of men, and it grows and flowers, and then it must die." And sometimes I think that Lawrence was the last green shoot on the tree of English civilization. Anyhow, whether English civilization is dead or not, and I hope it isn't, Lawrence is the last shoot of it that has grown ahead and pierced the air.

He was always so absolutely, undeniably, *something*. "They can't ignore me in the long run," he would say, with clenched teeth, "they can't get past me, much as they'd like to." And I think they can't.

Life rattles on so mechanically, there is less and less meaning in its motor-hoots and in all the noise, all meaning is drowned. Nobody has delicate courage enough to listen to the things that give us genuine vibrating life. Our feelers for life, just quick life, are atrophied.

When I think that nobody wanted Lawrence's amazing genius, how he was jeered at, suppressed, turned into nothing, patronized at best, the stupidity of our civilization comes home to me. How necessary he was! How badly needed! Now that he is dead and his great love for his fellowmen is no longer there in the flesh, people sentimentalize over him. . . . Critics indeed! Had they been able to *take* instead of criticizing, how much richer their own lives might have been!

Those wonderful mornings in our little podere, getting up joyfully to that Mediterranean sun by the sea! And I'd walk through the olive trees to Telaro, for the post. It took me, the northerner, some time to see the beauty of these olive trees, so different at different times; the wind running up them turns them into quicksilver and sometimes they seem quite tired and still and dark. During those early morning walks the sun threw delicate quivering shadows on the stony, mossy path. To my right was the sea. I wouldn't have been surprised meeting Christ and his disciples—it may be just as well that I didn't.

Lawrence could well teach people how to live, how to be grateful simply for life itself. He who was always so frail and so much nearer death at every moment than most people, how religiously he appreciated every good moment! Every big and little thing! I hadn't lived before I lived with Lawrence. It was drudgery, grey tired days with endless efforts, before. With him, being in love and ecstasy was only a small part of the whole, always the whole and we two balanced in it, the universe around us for us to take as much as we could, and we took a lot of it in those eighteen years together.

Of his short life didn't Lawrence make the most! It was his deep sense of the reality of living. He knew what feeds the life-flame in a creature, it isn't Rolls-Royces or first-class hotels and cinemas. He wasn't a high-brow and he wasn't a low-brow, but with real genius he got out of the quick of living the abiding values and said so in his writing. It is always amazing to me how little people understand him. Misunderstand him, is more like it.

I suppose when you are inside the pale you see only the palings and think they are quite splendid, but once outside, you realize how big the world is and the palings are just palings to you. You look at them in surprise: all these insurmountable obstacles, it was only rather low palings to climb over after all. But for those who feel safe inside, let them, the palings don't care, neither does the bigger world.

He was quite aware of the hostility to him, but in those days I don't think we either of us measured the depth of it. Also, as he grew more and more, the antagonism grew. We were too busy living to take much notice. Our own world, so small and poor to others on the outside, what a strong, unconquerable fortress it really was!

Another thing I understood: there was no "God-Almightiness" about him, like the universal "I-am-everlasting" feeling of Goethe, for instance. He knew "I am D. H. Lawrence from my head to my toes, and there I begin and there I end and my soul lives inside me. All else is not me, but I can have a relationship with all that is not me in the world, and the more I realize the otherness of other things around me the richer I am."

It makes me laugh when I think of that American doctor who "looked at literature" who wrote about Lawrence and saw only a diseased prurient mind in him. I think all he wanted to see was disease. Because Ursula, and Birkin, in "Women in Love," have a good meal with beetroot and ham and venison pastry, he reads some horror into beetroot and ham and pastry. I think the horror was in the good doctor's mind, for what horror is there in beetroot or ham or venison pastry? Good to eat they are, that's all. Lawrence was so direct, such a real puritan! He hated any "haut-goût" or lewdness. Fine underclothing and all the apparatus of the seducing sort were just stupid to him. All tricks; why tricks? Passionate people don't need tricks.

❧❧❧

In the spring of 1914 Lawrence and I went from Fiaschetino to London. We stayed with a friend, Gordon Campbell, whose wife was in Ireland. The house was in Kensington. We saw a good deal of the Murrys and there were long discussions between us all. Katherine was young and yet old, like a precocious child. I never suspected so much sadness in her, then; her relation with Murry seemed so fresh and young.

We had a housekeeper, Mrs. Conybear, who sang "Angels ever bright and fair" from the basement.

Campbell was very much in love with Ireland, "Areland" he called it. At breakfast always sad and cross, about "Areland."

I remember a ghastly Sunday afternoon when we wanted to amuse ourselves. We went on one of the Thames boats to Richmond—Campbell, Murry, Katherine, Lawrence and I—there were a few seedy people on the boat—a sad object of a man was playing "Lead, Kindly Light" on a harmonium—we got more and more silent with the dreariness of that enjoyment. And then, further along, people threw sixpences from the boat into that centuries-old, awful-looking Thames mud and small boys dived for them—the Thames mud seemed to soak into our very souls and soon we could not stand it any more and left the boat and got a bus to go home. Campbell, a dignified person, trod on the conductor's toe going on top and the conductor said: "Hallo, clumsy," to Katherine's and my joy.

Finally I and Lawrence got married at a registrar's office in Kensington. Campbell and Murry went with us. On the way there Lawrence dashed out of the cab into a goldsmith's to buy a new wedding ring. I gave my old one to Katherine and with it she now lies buried in Fontainebleau.

It was quite a simple and not undignified ceremony. I didn't care whether I was married or not, it didn't seem to make any difference, but I think Lawrence was glad that we were respectable married people.

On that first visit to London Lawrence's writings were already a little known and I thought: "What fun it is going to be to know some amusing people." But then, oh dear, we were asked to lunch by a few lion huntresses and the human being in me felt only insulted. You were fed more or less well, you sat next to somebody whose name had also been printed in the papers, the hostess didn't know who or what you were, thought you were somebody else, and wanted to shoo you away after you were fed like chickens that had become a nuisance, and that was all. So Lawrence and I hardly went anywhere. What fun people might have had with us they never realized; perhaps they had no fun in themselves. So Lawrence and I were mostly alone.

A friend asked me once: "But wasn't it very difficult, Lawrence and you coming from a different class, wasn't the actual contact very difficult, wasn't your sensitiveness offended?"

I don't know whether it was the genius in Lawrence or the man from the people in him, but I certainly found him more delicately and sensitively aware of me than I ever imagined anybody would be.

Once I bumped my head against a shutter and was a little stunned and Lawrence was in such an agony of sympathy and tenderness over it. It astonished me; when I had bumped my head before or hurt myself nobody seemed to bother and I didn't see why they should have done so. To be so enveloped in tenderness was a miracle in itself for me.

The War

AND THEN the war came, quite out of the blue for us both. Lawrence was on a walking tour in the Lakes with two friends and I was in London. After Lawrence came back, I remember our having lunch with Rupert Brooke and Eddie Marsh. I see Rupert Brooke's strange fair skin, he blushed so easily, the beauty of him was strangely sad. He was coming to stay with us. Even then I thought: "He has had enough of life, it wearies him." He wasn't a bit happy or fulfilled. I remember Eddie Marsh saying: "There will be war, we fear, but it may be that the Foreign Office and Earl Grey have averted it today."

But we couldn't believe it. . . . War. . . .

But Winston Churchill had only said: "Bloody peace again."

And then it was declared. At first it seemed only exciting. . . . Exciting indeed! Nobody realized at first what hell, what lowest demons, had been let loose.

We were at Charing Cross station and saw trains of soldiers depart. Their women were there so pale and strained-looking, saying good-bye, trying to be brave and not cry. It made me weep for those unknown women and their sorrow. What did I care whether these boys, boys so many of them, were English or Russian or French. Nationality was just an accident and here was grief. Lawrence was ashamed of my tears.

He himself was bewildered and lost, became abstract and

mental, and couldn't feel any more. I, who had been brought up with all the "big-drumming" of German militarism, I was scared.

Lawrence was not a pacifist, he fought all his life. But that "World War" he condemned with all his might. The inhuman, mechanical, sheer destruction of it! Destruction for what end!

Then when Lloyd George came to power Lawrence lost all hope in the spirit of his native country. Lloyd George, who was so un-English, to stand for English prestige! It seemed incredible.

War, more war! "Dies irae, dies illa," a monstrous disaster, the collapse of all human decency. Lawrence felt it so. I could feel only fear—all base instincts let loose, all security gone.

We were in a big crowd on Hampstead Heath one evening going home from a friend's house. In the sky, uncertain and terrible amidst the clouds, hung a Zeppelin. "In that Zeppelin," I thought, "are perhaps men I have danced with when I was a girl, boys I have played with, and here they come to bring destruction and death. And if this dark crowd knew I was a German they would tear me to pieces in their fear."

Sadly we went home. So helpless we were, at the power of all horrors. We took a small cottage out in Berkshire. Suspicion was ever present. Even when we were gathering blackberries in the nearby hedges a policeman popped up behind a bush and wanted to know who we were. Lawrence, who comes out in the open so courageously in his writings, why, why, do so many people see a sinister figure in him? The darkness wasn't in him but in those others. There is a woman even now who boasts that she turned us out of Cornwall as spies.

Our cottage was near the mill of Gilbert and Mary Cannan. And the Murrys were an hour's walk away in another cottage. We would go over to them in the dark winter nights, through bare woods and fields of dead cabbage stalks, with their smell of rottenness.

Campbell came to spend a weekend with us. He, who in London had been so elegant, with spats and top-hat, now wore an old cap and carried a very heavy stick under his arm. He looked to me like an Irish tramp. He was still weeping over his "Areland."

Christmas came. We made the cottage splendid with holly and mistletoe, we cooked and boiled, roasted and baked. Campbell and Koteliansky and the Murrys came, and Gertler and the Cannans. We had a gay feast.

We danced on the shaky floor. Gilbert with uplifted head sang: "I feel, I feel like an eagle in the sky." Koteliansky sang soulfully his Hebrew song: "Ranani Sadekim Badanoi." Katherine, with a long, ridiculous face, sang this mournful song:

I am an unlucky man,
I fell into a coalhole
I broke my leg,
And got three months for stealing coal.
I am an unlucky man,
If it rained soup all day,
I wouldn't have a spoon,
I'd only have a fork.

She also sang:

Ton sirop est doux, Madeleine,
Ton sirop est doux.
Ne crie pas si fort, Madeleine,
La maison n'est pas à nous.

I liked this tune, but when I sang it Lawrence stopped me; it was too "fast" for him. This occasion was the last time for years to come that we were really gay.

In the spring we went to stay with the Meynells in Sussex. We were fond of all the sons and daughters. Monica was our neighbour. We lived in the cottage that Violet had lent us. I only remember Alice Meynell as a vision in the distance, being led by Wilfred Meynell across the lawn like Beatrice being led by Dante.

I heard while there of my father's death. I did not tell anybody, I kept it to myself. When I told Lawrence he only said: "You didn't expect to keep your father all your life?" Bertrand Russell invited Lawrence to Cambridge at that time. Lawrence had expected much of this visit. "What did you do there? What did they say?" I asked him, when he came back.

He answered: "Well, in the evening they drank port and they walked up and down the room and talked about the Balkan situation and things like that, and they know nothing about it."

We had met Lady Ottoline Morrell. She was a great influence in Lawrence's life. Her profound culture, her beautiful home, "Garsington," her social power, all meant much to Lawrence.

I felt in those days: "Perhaps I ought to leave Lawrence to her influence; what might they not do together for England? I am powerless, and a Hun, and a nobody." Garsington was a refuge during the war for many people and stood as a stronghold for freedom in those unfree days.

Later we took a small flat in the Vale of Heath. "The Rainbow" appeared and was suppressed. When it happened I felt as though a murder had been done, murder of a new, free utterance on the face of the earth. I thought the book would be hailed as a joyous relief from the ordinary dull stuff, as a way out into new and unknown regions. With his whole struggling soul Lawrence had written it. Then to have it condemned, nobody standing for it—the bitterness of it! He was sex-mad, they said. Little even now do people realize what men like Lawrence do for the body of life, what he did to rescue the fallen angel of sex. Sex had fallen in the gutter, it had to be pulled out. What agony it was to know the flame in him and see it quenched by his fellowmen! "I'll never write another word I mean," he said in his bitterness; "they aren't fit for it," and for a time the flame in him was quenched.

It could not be for long; I remember with joy A. S. Frere-Reeves' words: "Lawrence is like a man so far ahead on the road, that he seems small." When I think of his critics the words of Heraclitus come into my mind:

"The Ephesians would do well to hang themselves, every grown man of them, and leave the city to beardless lads, for they have cast out Hermodorus, the best man among them, saying: 'We will have none who is best among us; if there be any such, let him be so elsewhere and among others.' "

The best were treated so during the war. And in those dark days I had a bad time. Naturally, I came in for all Lawrence's tortured, irritable moods. His sweetness had disappeared and he turned against me as well as the rest for the time being. It all made him ill. There was not even a little hope or gaiety anywhere. We had a little flat in the Vale of Heath in Hampstead. He didn't like the Vale of Heath and he didn't like the little flat and he didn't like me or anybody else. . . . And the war was everywhere. . . . We were saturated with war.

Cornwall

At Cornwall, near Zennor, we found Tregerthen cottage. As usual we made it out of a granite hole into a livable place. It cost five pounds a year rent. We had made it very charming. We washed the walls very pale pink and the cupboards were painted a bright blue. This was the entrance room; all very small but well proportioned.

There was a charming fireplace on which lived two Staffordshire figures riding to market, "Jasper and Bridget." On the wall was a beautiful embroidery Lady Ottoline Morrell had embroidered after a drawing by Duncan Grant, a tree with big bright flowers and birds and beasts. Behind the sitting room was a darkish rough scullery, and upstairs was one big room overlooking the sea, like the big cabin on the upper deck of a ship. And how the winds from that untamed Cornish sea rocked the solid little cottage, and howled at it, and how the rain slashed it, sometimes forcing the door open and pouring into the room.

I see Katherine Mansfield and Murry arriving sitting on a cart, high up on all the goods and chattels, coming down the lane to Tregerthen. Like an emigrant Katherine looked. I loved her little jackets, chiefly the one that was black and gold like bees.

It was great fun buying very nicely made furniture for a few shillings in St. Ives, with the Murrys. The fishermen were selling their nice old belongings to buy modern stuff. Our purchases would arrive tied on a shaky cart with bits of rope, the cart trundling down the uneven road. I think our best buy was a well-proportioned bedstead we got for a shilling. Then in both the Murrys' neighbouring cottage and our own such a frenzy broke out of painting chairs and polishing brass and mending old clocks, putting plates on the dressers, arranging all the treasures we had bought. After they had settled in their cottage I loved walking with Katherine to Zennor. A high wind she hated and stamped her foot at it. Later we'd sit in the sun under the foxgloves and talk, like two Indian braves, as she said. We enjoyed doing things together. I can see her round eyes when Murry painted all the chairs black with Ripolin and she said: "Look at the funereal procession of chairs." She told me many things from her life, but she told me them in confidence and trust.

Katherine and Lawrence and Murry had invented a place, a wonderful place where we were all going to live in complete bliss; Rananim it was called.

Lawrence thought of the new spirit of the life we would try to live there. Murry thought of the ship, and its equipment, that would take us to our island of Rananim. Katherine saw all the coloured bundles that we would have to take. By the hour we could talk Rananim.

There in Cornwall I can remember days of complete harmony between the Murrys and us, Katherine coming to our cottage so thrilled at my foxgloves, tall in the small window seat. Since then whenever I see foxgloves I must think of Katherine.

One day we went out on the sea in bright sunshine in a boat, and sang the canon:

Row, row, row your boat
Gently down the stream,
Merrily, merrily, merrilv, merrily,
Life is but a dream.

I don't know why even then this canon moved me so. They were so strangely significant, those words. And I was so bad at keeping my part of the song going, to Lawrence's rage.

So much, so much was still ahead for us all. And all so wonderful. At that time we were so poor, and such nobodies, and yet so rich in dreams and gaiety! But then Lawrence would have his reactions against all this, feel that his dreams were like petty vapourings, that the only real facts were war, and a war of all the lower elements come uppermost, carrying all before them. Grimly his soul would try to understand, but in the end it could only hang on to its faith, to its own, own, unknown God.

He had to go through with it, that I knew; also I knew—however miserable I was, and he made me so—that there was a man who suffered because of his vision.

He wanted people to be as they came out of the hands of the Lord, not to violate them but gently adjust them to life in their own capacity. He didn't expect me to type, I hated it. Poor as we were he never expected me to do it. "People should do what they enjoy, then they'll do it well," he said.

In the first year of the war Cornwall was still not quite engulfed by it; but slowly, like an octopus, with slow but dead-sure tentacles, the war spirit crept up and all around us. Suspicion and fear surrounded us. It was like breathing bad air and walking on a bog.

I remember once sitting on the rocks with Lawrence, by the sea, near our cottage at Tregerthen. I was intoxicated by the air and sun. I had to jump and run, and my white scarf blew in the wind. "Stop it, stop it, you fool, you fool!" Lawrence cried. "Can't you see they'll think that you're signalling to the enemy!"

I had forgotten the war for a moment.

There was an unfortunate policeman from St. Ives. He had to trot up so many times to our cottage to look over and over again Lawrence's papers, to see if he were really an Englishman and his father without a doubt an Englishman, and if his mother was English. This policeman once said to me: "Oh, ma'am, if I dare only speak my thoughts, but I mustn't." But he took the peas and beans I offered him from our field that Lawrence had ploughed with the help of William Henry from the farm, and sown with vegetables. They came up splendidly and lots of people had vegetables from this field during the war.

Out standby and friend was Katie Berryman. Her saffron cake and baked stuffed rabbit were our modest luxuries.

We had so little money, Lawrence not being wanted, nor his work, in those days when profiteers and such men were flourishing and triumphant. I remember his writing to Arnold Bennett and saying: "I hear you think highly of me and my genius, give me some work."

Arnold Bennett wrote back: "Yes, I do think highly of your genius, but that is no reason why I should give you work."

The war seemed to drive Lawrence to utter despair. He was called up for inspection and told me about it afterwards. "You have no idea what a pathetic sight all the men were in nothing but their shirts." How glad he was to come back to his cottage and me!

Lawrence was fond of the people at Tregerthen Farm nearby. Their Celtic natures fascinated him. He could talk by the hour with William Henry, the farmer's elder son, ruddy and handsome.

In those days Lawrence seemed to turn against me, perhaps on account of the bit of German in me. I felt utterly alone there, on that wild Cornish moor, in the little granite cottage. Often Lawrence would leave me in the evenings, and go over to the farm, where he'd spend his time talking to William Henry and giving French lessons to Stanley, the younger son.

Sometimes at night, in the dark, the door would fly open, and it seemed as if the ancient spirits and ghosts of the place blew into my cottage. In the loneliness I seemed to hear the voices of young men crying out to me from the battlefields: "Help us, help us, we are dying, we are dying." Despair had blown in on the night. I thought how in the past women like Catherine of Siena had influenced events. But now what could any woman do to stem or divert this avalanche?

And then Lawrence would come home and want to quarrel with me, as if he were angry with me because I too felt sad and hopeless and helpless.

It was only at the very last, and out of one's final despair, that there arose a hope and a belief. But the outer world was viler every day.

I remember coming home from Zennor with a loaf of Katie Berryman's bread in Lawrence's rucksack. Coastguards suddenly pounced on us from behind a hedge and said: "Let us look at your rucksack, you have a camera in there."

I could feel Lawrence swooning with rage. I opened the rucksack and held the loaf of bread under their noses. I had to show my contempt, if they hanged me for it the next moment. I believe they would have liked to.

It was no wonder Lawrence went almost mad at times at the creeping foulness around us; he, who came out so completely in the open. And I knew that he felt so helpless, as if all that he believed in was utterly lost, he who by his genius felt responsible for the spirit of his England, he whose destiny it was to give England a new direction.

If only the war could end! But it went on, was present wherever you went, there was no escaping it. One evening at Cecil Grey's place, Bosigran Castle, we were sitting after dinner, when there came a knock at the door and four coast-watchers stood there ominously.

"You are showing a light."

To Grey's dismay it was true. He had a new housekeeper from London and the light from her bedroom could be seen at sea.

As we stood there I shivered with alarm. I had before this been under suspicion of giving supplies to the German submarine crews. As for the suspicion, we were so poor at the time—a biscuit a day we might have spared for the submarines, but no more.

I took a secret pleasure in the fact that our coast-watchers were all covered with mud. They had fallen into a ditch listening under the windows.

Fortunately Grey had an uncle who was an admiral. That saved him, and us. As for Lawrence, he just looked at those men. What a manly job theirs was, listening under other people's windows!

A few days later I came home from Bosigran Castle to the cottage. Lawrence was away, had driven to Penzance. In the dusk I entered the cottage alone. Immediately I was inside I knew by instinct something had happened, I felt overwhelming fear. With shaking knees I went to the farm. Yes, I was told, two men had asked for us.

I was full of foreboding, even though Lawrence, coming home later, didn't share my fear.

But then early next morning there appeared a captain, two detectives, and my friend the policeman. The captain read us a paper that we must leave the county of Cornwall in three days. Lawrence, who lost his temper so easily, was quite calm.

"And what is the reason," he asked.

"You know better than I do," answered the captain.

"I don't know," said Lawrence.

Then the two awful detectives went through all our cupboards, clothes, beds, etc., while I, like a fool, burst into a rage:

"This is your English liberty, here we live and don't do anybody any harm, and these creatures have the right to come here and touch our private things."

"Be quiet," said Lawrence.

He was so terribly quiet, but the iron of his England had stabbed his soul once more, and I knew he suffered more than I.

In the background stood my friend the policeman, full of sympathy. How sad I was, and desperate. But nothing could be done, so we left Cornwall, like two criminals. When we were turned out of Cornwall something changed in Lawrence for ever.

We went to London where H.D. lent us her flat in Mecklenburg Square. It had a very large room. Richard Aldington was home on leave at the time and in the evening we met and were very gay.

Where did we get the courage to be gay? I don't know.

Lawrence invented wonderful charades. Once we played

the Garden of Eden. Lawrence was the Lord, H.D. was the tree, Richard Aldington waving a large chrysanthemum was Adam, and I was the serpent, and a little scared at my part.

A few days later Cynthia Asquith invited us to the royal box that Lady Cunard had lent her at Covent Garden.

Lawrence trimmed his beard, we made ourselves very fine, and went to listen to "Aïda."

Very few people wanted to be friendly to us in those days. I was a Hun and Lawrence not wanted.

That was the time of air raids over London, the time there was such a strain on people's nerves. During the air raids we were supposed to go into the cellar, but Lawrence always refused to go; he stayed in bed. And it certainly was very depressing being in the cellar with all the other gloomy people. So I spent my time during air raids running up and down stairs imploring Lawrence to come to the cellar. But he'd never do it.

We met Gertler in those days and he used to tell us funny stories about his experiences during air raids, especially one sudden one when he lost his head and kept running up and down the stairs of a strange house. Campbell also told about air raid experiences, how once in Hampstead Heath he'd found himself buried under a heap of terrified housemaids coming home from a dinner party.

Yet underneath all this gaiety, we were so dulled and bitter. "Dancing while Rome burns." But if Nero enjoyed his burning Rome, we did not. And Lawrence's helplessness to stem this lavaflood of death to all that is best in man made him savage underneath and again I had a bad time. . . . It was torture to live, and to live with him.

I felt helpless and an outcast, and only a burden and a difficulty for Lawrence.

I, the Hunwife in a foreign country!

Then we went to Hermitage in Berkshire. The country there is so quiet and English with its woods. Our simple life in the cottage healed him a lot.

I saw my son, who was in the O.T.C., and it seemed terrible that he would have to fight against his own relations, perhaps, and I said: "Let me hide you somewhere in a cave or in a wood, I don't want you to go and fight, I don't want you to be killed in this stupid war." But he was shocked.

All this time we were followed by detectives. Detectives had even gone to my first husband and asked him if he knew anything against me.

While we were there in Hermitage the armistice came. I nearly said peace came. But it was not peace, it is not peace yet. The war has bred not peace but awful gargoyle children of hate and resentment, and has only left death as the desirable, clean thing, almost.

Lawrence and My Mother

LAWRENCE AND my mother were fond of one another; she was a wonderful mother to us, her three daughters. We were all three different and yet she helped and understood us, and was there for us in our hours of need—alas, there were plenty of them for the three of us. But she was equal to all the awful situations we found ourselves in. My eldest sister Else wanted to study, when studying for women in Germany was still infra dig; I remember walking through the crowds of men students into a lecture hall at Heidelberg with my sister at sixteen and feeling like a real martyr. My sister Johanna had lovely names for my mother, like "Goldfasanchen," my little golden pheasant—it was so quaint to hear her, worldly and elegant, being so tender with my mother, and she half loving it and saying: "What do you want now?" She had taught me the love for poetry from early childhood. Especially after the war she and Lawrence became great friends. She lived in her "Stift," at Baden-Baden, a kind of home for women, mostly widows of distinguished men, Excellencies and so on. It was a very dignified life. We three sisters loved to meet there and stay with my mother. We had to be on our best behaviour, except in my mother's beautiful rooms, where all the wildness of our childhood came back, especially for my sister Johanna and me. Lawrence sat on the sofa, happily, while my mother tried to give him all the things for tea that he liked—"Pumpernickel" and "Trüffelleberwurst"—and we played wild games of bridge.

Sometimes, when Lawrence wanted to complain about me she would say: "I know her longer than you, I know her."

He wrote his "Fantasia of the Unconscious" in the woods behind the Altes Schloss. We stayed in a rough little inn at Ebersteinburg. I remember that we had some friends to dinner and a chicken flew into the soup tureen.

Then Lawrence, in the meagre after-the-war days, would scour the country for some cream for her.

She was very happy in Lawrence's life and mine, it meant so much to her, but she always trembled that the women in the Stift might read his books.

He was so polite to them and they liked him, again he was the Herr Doktor.

At Ebersteinburg he would go out in the morning and take his book and fountain-pen. I would find him later on, leaning against a big pine tree; it was as if the tree itself helped him to write his book, and poured its sap into it.

Then we would go down to Baden to my mother in the afternoon and take her our wildflowers or some honey or fruit or nuts; or we would go for long walks and make the place our own as usual. Looking over the Rheintal or listening to the music in the Kurpark. Baden was no longer the Baden of Turgeniev and archdukes and grand dukes and the Prince of Wales; no, it was after the war, would-be elegant.

Lawrence and my mother in her wisdom and ripeness understood each other so well. She said to me: "It's strange that an old woman can still be as fond of a man as I am of that Lorenzo."

Happy was their relationship. Only the last time, when my mother was so frail and old herself, being with Lawrence who was so very ill, they got on each other's nerves, and when she

FRIEDA'S MOTHER

saw him often so irritable with me, she said: "He isn't grateful to you for all you do for him." But I did not feel like that myself; I was glad to do everything for him I possibly could. It seemed little enough.

Then when she and I were going to meet for the first time after his death, we were afraid to meet. She knew what his death meant to me and I what it meant to her. So we avoided our common grief; there was no need of words.

I remember after she had been indoors for weeks, coming to Baden and taking her out on one of those first tender spring days we get in the north, just the first whisper of spring. To feel her respond to this coming renewal of the earth in an almost sacred happiness was very moving to me.

I think after Lawrence's death her desire to live left her. Less than a year after he died telling me: "You have many friends, you have much to live for yet," I got a telegram: "Come."

I went but it was too late. In the train I listened as it were to the sound of the wheels: "Is she still alive? Is she dead?" At the door of the Stift I was told: "The Frau Baronin died two hours ago."

She lay for the last time in her bedroom, the rocks of the Altes Schloss looking in through the window. "Lawrence is there for me," she had said. We, her three daughters, stood by her bedside, she for the first time not welcoming me with open arms as always. She lay with her silver hair like thistledown, in gentle and peaceful death.

She who had sustained our lives for half a century with the strength and harmony of her nature.

I remember my mother saying to me once: "But it's always you in Lorenzo's books, all his women are you." There was an expression on her face I could not get. Is she pleased at this or is she not? My sister Nusch was the only person that ever could take a liberty with him. She could lightly jump on his knee and say in her broken English:

"O Lorenzo, you are so nice, I like your red beard." He felt happy in the atmosphere of my mother and of us three sisters, so free and open and gay. Only when my sister Nusch and I had our long female talks, he did not like it, he had to be in it.

We spent some weeks at Zell-am-See with Nusch, her husband and children at her villa. We bathed and boated and Lawrence wrote his "Captain's Doll" there.

One day the peasants from my sister's shooting-lodge high up in the mountains brought us some honey and left. The honey was found to be full of worms. "Hadu," said Lawrence, full of rage, to my nephew, "you and I will take this honey back to them." So up they marched to the lodge, in the heat of the afternoon, Lawrence and Hadu, and arrived at the peasant's hut to find them in the midst of a meal; in the very middle of the table Lawrence planted the jar of honey and left without a word. The peasants remained petrified. "If honesty, common and garden honesty goes," Lawrence told me once, "then all is lost, life becomes impossible."

After the War

The first snow has fallen, it's a still, black and white world. All the gold of the autumn has gone. On the mountains it was green-gold where the aspens turned, and the oakbrush was red-gold and there was yellow-gold in the tall sunflowers all along the road to Taos. The sage brush bloomed pale yellow and the fields and openings of the woods were yellow with small sunflowers. The mountains looked like tigers with their stripes of gold and dark pine trees. And the golden autumn sun lit it all. Now it has gone, this golden world: the frost and the snow have taken it away. I am writing in the sun on the snowy hill behind the cabins, where the Indians had their camp; where Lawrence and I slept in the summer, years ago, and again a grey squirrel scolded me for intruding; I wonder if it is the same grey squirrel. The snow drips from the cedar trees that are alive with birds; it is melting fast; in the desert below it has gone. The pinto ponies look bright like painted wooden toys against the snow. The black and white pigs follow me grunting and the black cats look shiny and black on the whiteness, delicately trotting after me. I have seen tracks of wild turkeys, of deer and bears, in the Gallina. I am now leaving that English autumn there in Berkshire, with its blackberry hedges and mushroom fields and pale sunsets behind a filigree of trees.

I am leaving Lawrence behind, who doesn't want to come to Germany so soon after the war. I go on my journey, a nightmare of muddle, my trunks stolen. I arrive in Baden, so glad to see my sisters and my mother, but, oh, so many, many dead that had been our life and our youth. A sad, different Germany.

We had suffered so much, all of us, lost so much. And money was scarce.

Meanwhile Lawrence had gone to Florence and I went to join him. I arrived at four o'clock in the morning. "You must come for a drive with me," he said, "I must show you this town." We went in an open carriage, I saw the pale crouching Duomo and in the thick moonmist the Giotto tower disappeared at the top into the sky. The Palazzo Vecchio with Michelangelo's David and all the statues of men, we passed. "This is a men's town," I said, "not like Paris, where all statues are women." We went along the Lungarno, we passed the Ponte Vecchio, in that moonlight night, and ever since Florence is the most beautiful town to me, the lily town, delicate and flowery.

Lawrence was staying at a pensione on the Lungarno with Norman Douglas and Magnus.

The English there in Florence had still a sense of true hospitality, in the grand manner. And yet it struck me all as being like "Cranford" only it was a man's "Cranford." And the wickedness there seemed like old maids' secret rejoicing in wickedness. Corruption is not interesting to me, nor does it frighten me: I find it dull.

Nobody knows Norman Douglas that doesn't know him in German. When he talks German you know something about him that you don't know if you only know him in English. I was thrilled at the fireworks of wit that went off between Lawrence and Douglas. They never quarrelled. I understood that

Douglas had to stand up for his friend Magnus and to Lawrence's logical puritanical mind Magnus presented a problem of human relations. When we had gone to Capri and Magnus was in trouble at Montecassino, Lawrence went there and lent him some money, and yet we had so very little then.

Later Magnus appeared at our Fontana Vecchia at Taormina, having fled from Montecassino. He came almost taking for granted that we would be responsible for him, that it was our duty to keep him. This disturbed Lawrence.

"Is it my duty to look after this man?" he asked me.

To me it was no problem. Had I been fond of Magnus, had he had any meaning, or purpose—but no, he seemed only anti-social, a poor devil without any pride, and he didn't seem to matter anyhow. With the money Lawrence had lent him, he stayed at the best hotel in Taormina, to my great resentment, we who could not afford to stay even in a second-rate hotel. I felt he made a fool of Lawrence, and afterwards, when we went to Malta, crossing second class from Palermo, whom should I discover gaily swanking and talking to an English Navy officer but Magnus on the first-class deck! The cheek of the man! He had written to Lawrence: "I am sweating blood till I am out of Italy." I knew his sort, people always sweating blood and always going to shoot themselves. But Magnus, anyhow, did commit suicide at the end. It was a shock, but there was nothing else for him to do. It seemed to me he had put his money on the wrong horse. He thought the splendour of life lay in drinking champagne, having brocade dressing gowns, and that kind of thing. But Lawrence felt deeply disturbed by Magnus and did feel a responsibility for him.

There is a letter from Douglas to Lawrence in which Douglas says: "Go ahead, my boy, do as you like with Magnus's work." Lawrence wanted to pay the Maltese young men who had helped Magnus, hence the publication of Magnus's memoirs with Lawrence's introduction.

From Florence we went to Capri. I didn't like Capri; it was so small an island, it seemed hardly capable to contain all the gossip that flourished there. So Lawrence went to Sicily and took Fontana Vecchia for us, outside Taormina.

Living in Sicily after the war years was like coming to life again. Fontana Vecchia was a very simple but big-roomed villa.

Here are letters of Lawrence to my mother:

FONTANA VECCHIA
TAORMINA
SICILIA
16 MARCH

Meine liebe Schwiegermutter:

Your post card came this morning. I do hope you will be feeling better. Frieda is in Rome, doing her passport. I hope by the time you have this card she will be with you. It will make her happy to nurse you and get you better. Soon you must be about walking—and then I will come to Germany and perhaps we can all go away into the Schwarzwald and have a good time. Meanwhile I sit in Fontana Vecchia, and feel the house very empty without F. Don't like it at all: but don't mind so long as you will be better.

I am having my portrait painted: hope that today will be the last sitting, as I am tired. I look quite a sweet young man, so you will feel quite pleasant when I send you a photograph. The weather is once more sunny and beautiful, the sea so blue, and the flowers falling from the creeper.

I have no news as yet from F. from Rome, but hope she is managing everything easily. I am all right in Taormina: people invite me to tea and dinner all the time. But I don't want to go very badly. I am correcting the MS. of my diary of a Trip to Sardinia, which I think will amuse you. Give my love to Else. Tell me if there is anything I can send: and do get better soon.

D. H. L.

FONTANA VECCHIA
TAORMINA, SICILY
SUNDAY, DEC. 10

Dear Mother-in-Law:

I am glad you got the cheque. But don't trouble about being grateful. The money is there, all right, and enough said.

Frieda does not want any. We had a piece of luck. The professor of English Literature in Edinburgh gave me a prize: a hundred pounds for "The Lost Girl." That is *a piece of luck. I hope to have the money next week. A hundred pounds is a nice little sum.*

Please, mother-in-law, send 500 marks to Hadu and the rest.

We don't send any Christmas parcels, the post is so difficult here in Italy. But when the book arrives I will send it to you. I am so glad that you are feeling well. But go carefully before Xmas. Go on still, small feet and don't get overbearing and drunk.

D. H. L.

A thousand white horses on the hard blue sea and the sailing ships run anxiously with half a wing.

Frieda has made a hundred good "Seckerle," very good—made them this morning.

(Translated from the German)

Fontana Vecchia

I am not working at the present time. I wrote three long stories since we are here—that will make quite a nice book. I also collected my short stories ready for a book. So, for the moment I am free, I don't want to begin anything else, only perhaps translate a grey Sicilian novel "Maestro Don Gesualdo" by Giovanni Verga. It is pure Sicilian and you can see in it how heavy and black and hopeless are these Sicilians inside. Outside so beautiful, inside horror and money. No, mother-in-law, here out of Europe nothing new can come forth. They can only go on chewing the same old strings. The Banca di Sconto, perhaps the biggest bank in Italy, has failed, does not pay and such a black cloud over the people here. Money is the blood of an Italian. He says it himself: "Vuole il sangue mio—he wants my blood," if he has to pay. But it is also cruel. Very likely the Government will come and help the people. . . .

(Translated from the German)

Fontana Vecchia
Taormina
Sicily

Dear Mother-in-Law:

We must find a good ship. Maybe we'll leave next month, but not for sure. And if we go to America and I can earn some money, we can easily return to Germany and see you. If one only has the dollars, then America is no further from Baden than Taormina, perhaps not as far. You know it well.

I have had a little influenza, it was very cold, the snow came nearer and nearer down the mountains. Monte Venere was white, also our own Monte Riretto. But right near to us the snow could not reach, the sea said no, and now, thank God, it is warm as summer, the snow has flown away, the sea is blue, and the almonds are busy flowering. Many thousands of birds came down with the cold—goldfinches, blackbirds, redbreasts, red-tails, so gay and coloured, and thank goodness, cartridges are so dear that the Italians can't buy them.

Frieda also wants to write a word. We sit in the salotto, warm and still, with the lamp on the table. Outside, through the door, I see like twilight, the moonlit sea; and the moon through the begonia leaves of our terrace; and all quite still, except from time to time the stove crackles. If I think that we are going away I feel melancholy. But inside I feel sure, that I must go. This is a beautiful end, but better a difficult beginning than only an end.

Greet all. Tell Else I had all the letters: and Friedel writes

English so well. He'll think little of my German. I am so glad you have Annie with you and are not alone these long winter evenings.

Keep well always. I'll write again soon. Make a bow for me to all the ladies of the Stift in my name.

Your son-in-law,

D. H. LAWRENCE

(Translated from the German)

Fontana Vecchia
Taormina
Sicily
Sunday

My dear Mother-in-Law:

We sit waiting to depart—4 trunks—one household trunk, 1 book trunk, Frieda's and mine, two small valises, a hatbox, and two very small bags: just like Abraham going to a new land. My heart is trembling now, mostly with pain—the going away from home and the people and Sicily. But I will forget it and only think of palms and elephants and monkeys and peacocks. Tomorrow at 10:34 we leave here: eat at Messina, where we must change, arrive at 8:30 at Palermo, then to the Hotel Panormus where our friend lives. Thursday to Naples by boat, there at the Hotel Santa Lucia. Then on the S.S. "Osterley," Orient Line, to Ceylon. The ship goes on to Australia. You have the address—Ardnarce, Lake View Estate, Kandy, Ceylon. Think, it is only 14 days from Naples. We can always return quickly when we've had enough. Perhaps Else is right and we shall return to our Fontana. I don't say no: I don't say anything for certain. Today I go, tomorrow I return. So things go. I'll write again from Palermo if there's time. I think of you.

D. H. L.

(Translated from the German)

R.M.S. "OSTERLEY"
TUESDAY, 28 FEBRUARY

My dear Mother-in-Law:

We have been gone for two days. We left Naples Sunday evening, 8 o'clock. Monday morning at 8 o'clock we came through the Straits of Messina and then for hours we saw our Etna like a white queen or a white witch there standing in the sky so magic-lovely. She said to me, "You come back here," but I only said, "No," but I wept inside with grief, grief of separation. The weather is wonderful—blue sky, blue sea, still. Today we see no land, only the long thin white clouds where Greece lies. Later on we shall see Crete (Candia). We arrive on Thursday at Port Said. There this letter goes on land. We also for a few hours. Then we go through the Suez Canal and so into the Red Sea. This ship is splendid, so comfortable, so much room and not many passengers. The berths are not half taken. It is just like a real luxury hotel. In the morning at seven o'clock comes the steward with a cup of tea.—If you want to take a bath and if cold or hot or how. At 8 o'clock the breakfast gong rings and such a menu—cooked pears, porridge, fish, bacon, eggs, fried sausages, beefsteak, kidneys, marmalade, all there. Then afterwards one sits about, flirts or plays croquet. Eleven o'clock comes the steward with a cup of Bovril. One o'clock lunch—soup, fish, chicken or turkey, meat, entrées, always much too much. Four o'clock tea, 7 o'clock dinner. Ah no, one eats all the time. But you also have an appetite at sea, when it is still and so heavenly like now. I find it strange that it is so still, so quiet, so civilized. The people all so still and so easy and such a cleanliness, all so comfortable. Yes, it is better than Italy. The Italians are not good now, everything becomes base. Frieda caught a cold in Naples, and you ought to see how good the steward and stewardess are with her as she lies in bed. They come so quickly with tea or soda water or what she wants and always such gentle manners. After Italy it is extraordinary. Yes, civilization is a beautiful and fine thing if it only remains alive and does not become ennui. I can write to you again from Aden and then not again before Ceylon. Now I go down and see if Frieda has got up. Her cold is better today.

I am sorry you were not there to see us go on board at Naples, with trunks and bits and pieces—baskets of apples and oranges (gifts) and a long board that is a piece of a Sicilian wagon painted very gaily with two scenes out of the life of Marco Visconte. Else knows how beautiful are these Sicilian carts and the facchini are always crying: "Ecco la Sicilia—Ecco la Sicilia in viaggio per l'India!" For the moment a rivederci.

Frieda also ought to write a word. D. H. L.

The whole afternoon we have seen Crete with snow on the mountains—so big the island. Also another little island, all yellow and desert with great ravines. Now the sun is down, the rim of the sky red, the sea inky blue and the littlest, finest, sharpest moon that I ever saw. It is already quite warm.

WEDNESDAY

Today only warm and still. Seen no land—seagulls and two ships. Tomorrow morning we arrive at Port Said—letters must be posted tonight before 10 o'clock. D. H. L.

R.M.S. "Osterley"
Tuesday, 7 March
Arabian Sea

Dear Mother-in-Law:

Perhaps I can post this letter at Aden this evening, but we do not stop. We have come so far and so lovely. We stopped three hours in Port Said, and it was quite like the Thousand and One Nights. It was 9 o'clock in the morning, and the ladies of Port Said were all abroad shopping. Little black waddling heaps of black crêpe and two houri eyes between veil and mantle. Comic is the little peg that stands above the nose and keeps veil and head-cloth together. There came a charabanc with twenty black women parcels. Then one of the women threw back her veil and spat at us because we are ugly Christians. But you still see everything—beggars, water carriers, the scribe who sits with his little table, and writes letters, the old one who reads the Koran, the men who smoke their "chibouks" in the open café and on the pavement—and what people! Beautiful Turks, Negroes, Greeks, Levantines, Fellaheen, three Bedouins out of the desert like animals, Arabs, wonderful. We have taken coal on board, and then at midday off again into the Suez Canal, and that is very interesting. The Canal is eighty-eight miles long, and you can only travel five miles an hour. There you sit on this great ship and you feel really on land, slowly travelling on a still land ship. The shores are quite near, you can surely throw an orange at the Arabs that work on the shores. Then you see beautifully, wonderfully, the Sahara Wüste, *or desert—which do you say? The waterway goes narrow and alone through red-yellow sands. From time to time Arabs with camels work on the shores and keep on shouting "Hallo, Hallo" when the big ship passes so slowly. In the distance little sharp sand hills so red and pink-gold and sharp and the horizon sharp like a knife edge so clear. Then a few lonely palms, lonely and lost in the strong light, small, like people that have not grown very tall.*

Then again only sand, gold-pink and sharp little sand hills, so sharp and defined and clear, not like reality but a dream. Solemn evening came, and we so still, one thought we did not seem to move any more. Seagulls flew about like a sandstorm, and a great black bird of prey alone and cruel, so black between thousands of white screaming, quick flying sea birds. Then we came to the Dead Sea, flat seas that extend very far, and slowly the sun sank behind the desert with marvellous colours, and as the sun had set, then such a sky like a sword burning green and pink. Beautiful it was, I have never seen anything so super-human. One felt near to the doors of the old Paradise, I do not know how, but something only half human, something of a heaven with grey-browed, overbearing and cruel angels. The palm trees looked so little the angels should be much bigger and every one with a sword. Yes, it is a frontier country.

Next morning we were in the Red Sea. There stands Mount Sinai, red like old dried blood, naked like a knife and so sharp, so unnaturally sharp, like a dagger that has been dipped in blood and has dried long ago and is a bit rusty and is always there like something dreadful between man and his lost Paradise. All is Semitic and cruel, naked, sharp. No tree, no leaf, no life: the murderous will and the iron of the idea and ideal—iron will and ideal. So they stand, these dreadful shores of this Red Sea that is hot like an oven without air. It is a strange exit through this Red Sea—bitter. Behind lie finally Jerusalem, Greece, Rome and Europe, fulfilled and past—a great dreadful dream. It began with Jews and with Jews it ends. You should see Sinai, then you could know it. The ideal has been wicked against men and Jehovah is father of the ideal and Zeus and Jupiter and Christ are only sons. And God be praised Sinai and the Red Sea are past and consummated.

Yesterday morning we came through the Straits of Bab-el-Mandeb, again into the open. I am so glad that we came this way. Yesterday we always saw land—Arabia naked and desert but not so red and sharp and like dried blood. Today we see no land but later on we shall pass Cape Socrotra. This ship has gained fifteen hours. We are fifteen hours before time. Perhaps we arrive in Colombo on Sunday evening instead of Monday. It is very warm, but there is always air. The sea is covered with little white sea-horses, but the ship is still and sure. We have not had one single bad moment. All here on board so friendly and so good and comfortable. I work on the translation of Maestro Don Gesualdo and I let my inkpot fall on the deck. The "Osterley" shall wear my black sign for ever. At 11 o'clock in the morning we do not get Bovril any more, but ice cream. The women all wear colourful summer frocks. In the evening we dance. We see now the little flying fish. They are all silver and they fly like butterflies, so wee. There are also little black dolphins that run about like little black pigs.

Benediciti,

D. H. LAWRENCE

Fontana Vecchia had a large podere to it. Great "vasche" were on the rocky slope toward the sea, pools of green water to feed the lemon and orange trees. The early almond blossoms pink and white, the asphodels, the wild narcissi and anemones, all these we found during our walks, nothing new would escape Lawrence and we never got tired finding new treasures.

We went on a jolly expedition to Syracuse with Renée and John Juta and Insole. Trains had their own sweet way in Italy then and arrived when they felt like it. I remember being much impressed by how Renée Hansard, with the experience of a true colonial, was fortified with a hamper of food and a spirit lamp so we could have tea at any time.

She pulled out her embroidery with its wools from a neat little bag. She turned the railway car into a live little temporary home. The quarries of Syracuse impressed me much. Here at Syracuse the flower of the Athenian youth had been defeated; in these quarries the Greek men had been put to starve while the ladies of Syracuse took their walks along the top of the quarries to see them slowly die. A sinister dread impression it left in me. I doubt whether centuries can clean a place of such inhumanity, the place will retain and remember such horrors. Syracuse and its splendour have gone. Man is more cruel than nature but whenever he has been so he pays for it.

Of our winter excursion to Sardinia Lawrence has described every minute, it seems to me, with extraordinary accuracy.

Garibaldi, the picturesque, had begun his campaign here in Sicily with his thousand, with his Anita and his South American experience.

Along our rocky road the peasants rode past into the hills

on their donkeys, singing loudly, the shepherds drove their goats along, playing their reed pipes as in the days of the Greeks. We had an old Greek temple in the garden; there was the beautiful Greek theatre at Taormina, facing the Etna; what a marvellous stage for a play, not a modern play, alas, but how I longed to see one of the old giants like Sophocles there. How I longed for the old splendour of life to come back to us in those shabby after-the-war days.

"Give me a little splendour, O Lord," would be my prayer.

There in Taormina, in the whole of Sicily, one could feel the touch of the hands of many civilizations: Greek and Moorish and Norman and beyond into the dim past.

Old Grazia did our shopping and I loved watching Lawrence doing the accounts with her, her sly old Sicilian face spying his, how much she could rook him.

"She can rook me a little, but not too much," he would say, and he kept a firm hand on her.

The sun rose straight on our beds in the morning, we had roses all winter and we lived the rhythm of a simple life, getting up early, he writing or helping in the house or getting the tangerines from the round little trees in the garden or looking at the goat's new kids. Eating, washing up, cleaning the floor and getting water from the trough near the wall, where the large yellow snake came to drink and drew itself into its hole in the wall again.

Wherever Lawrence was, the surroundings came alive so intensely. At the Fontana Vecchia we mostly cooked on charcoal fires, but on Sundays he lit the big kitchen stove for me, and I, who had become quite a good cook by now, made cakes and tarts, big and little, sweet pies and meat pies and put them on the side-board in the dining room and called them Mrs. Beeton's show.

Once we had lunch with three friends at their villa. It was a jolly lunch. We had had some white wine that seemed innocent, but it was not. When we left, going home, I felt its effects but soon got over it.

"We must hurry, because those two English ladies are coming to tea."

So we hurried home and unfortunately the white Sicilian wine affected Lawrence later. The very English ladies came and Lawrence was terribly jovial and friendly with them. I tried to pull his sleeve and whispered: "Go away," but it was no use.

"What are you telling me to go away for?" he said.

I could see the two visitors being very uneasy and wanting to leave.

"No, no, you must have some mimosa, I'll get you some," Lawrence insisted. So he went with them through the garden, tried to climb a small mimosa tree and fell.

The ladies hurried away.

Next day Lawrence was chagrined and he met one of the ladies and tried to apologize to her, but she was very stiff with him, so he said: "Let her go to blazes."

I think from this incident arose the story that Lawrence was a drunkard. Poor Lawrence, he who could not afford wine and didn't want it, who was so naturally abstemious. I have seen him drunk only twice in all my life with him.

We stayed at Taormina in the heat and I remember when the mulberries were ripe and delicious and he climbed a big mulberry tree in his bathing suit. The mulberries were so juicy and red and they ran down his body so that he looked like one of those very realistic Christs we had seen on our walk across the Alps years ago.

He wrote "Birds, Beasts and Flowers" and "Sea and Sardinia" at Fontana Vecchia, and also "The Lost Girl." "Sea and Sardinia" he wrote straight away when we came back from Sardinia in about six weeks. And I don't think he altered a word of it. His other works, especially the novels, he wrote many times, parts of them anyhow. Sometimes I liked the first draft best, but he had his own idea and knew the form he wanted it to take.

One day I found the manuscript of "Sea and Sardinia" in the W.C. at Fontana Vecchia. So I told him: "But why did you put it there, it's such a pity, it's so nicely written and tidy." I had then no idea it might have any value, only regretted the evenly written pages having this ignominious end. But no, he had a passion for destroying his own writing. He hated the personal touch.

"I would like to burn all my writing. Print is different. They can have it in print, my stuff."

Just as he wanted Lawrence, the private person, separate from Lawrence the writer, the public man. He guarded his privacy ferociously. He liked best to meet people who knew nothing about him. He really disliked talking about his writing. "They don't like it, anyhow," he would say. But I read every day what he had written; his writing was the outcome of our daily life.

I had to take in what he had written and had to like it. Then he was satisfied and did not care for the approval of the rest of the world. What he wrote he had lived and was sure of. Travelling with him was living new experiences vividly every minute.

Then from Fontana Vecchia, we were really leaving Europe for the first time.

We did so much with the little money we had, making homes and unmaking them.

We unmade our beloved Fontana Vecchia and went to Palermo where the "facchini" were so wild and threw themselves on our luggage; I can see Lawrence struggling amongst a great crowd of them, waving his umbrella about, equally wild. It was midnight and I was terrified.

An American friend gave me the side of a Sicilian cart I had always longed for. It had a joust painted on one panel, on the other St. Genevieve. It was very gay and hard in colour. I loved it. Lawrence said: "You don't mean to travel to Ceylon with this object?"

"Let me, let me," I implored. So he let me. And off we set for Naples. There we were bounced in the harbour into our P. & O. boat. We arrived nearly too late, the gang-plank was pulled up immediately the minute we got on board. How we enjoyed that trip! Everybody feeling so free and detached, no responsibility for the moment, people going to meet husbands or wives, people going to Australia full of the wonders that were coming to them, and Lawrence being so interested and feeling so well. How tenderly one loves people on boats! They seem to become bosom friends for life. And then we went through the Suez Canal into the Red Sea, Arabia Deserta on one side, so very deserta, so terrifying. Then one morning I woke up and I was sure I could smell cinnamon; the ship stopped and we were in Colombo. It struck me: "I know it all, I know it all." It was just as I expected it. The tropics, so marvellous these black people, this violent quick growth and yet a little terrifying, a little repulsive, as Lawrence would say.

We stayed with the Brewsters in a huge bungalow with all those black servants in the background. In the morning the sun rose and we got up and I always felt terrified at the day and its heat. The sun rose higher and the heat would rise. We went for a walk and I saw a large thing coming towards us, large like a house, an elephant holding a large tree with its trunk! Its guide made him salaam to us, the great animal—young natives would come and pay visits to us and the Brewsters, who were interested in Buddhism. Lawrence became so terribly English and snubbed them mostly. Some young Cingalese said I had the face of a saint! Didn't I make the most of it and didn't Lawrence get this saint rubbed into him! Then we had the fantastic experience of a Pera-Hera given in honour of the Prince of Wales. Such a contrast was the elegant figure of the Prince sitting on the balcony of the Temple of the Tooth amongst the black seething tropical mass of men. The smell of the torches and the oily scent of dark men. Great elephants at midnight, and the heat in the dark. The noise of the tom-toms that goes right through some dark corner in one's soul. The night falls so quickly and the tom-toms begin and we could see the native fires on the hills all around. Noises from the jungle; those primeval cries and howls and the brain-fever bird and the sliding noises on the roof and the jumps in the darkness outside! How could one rest under such a darkness that was so terribly alive!

The climate didn't suit Lawrence and we had to leave. Lawrence was not well and happy in Ceylon. The tropics didn't suit him.

I was so enthralled with the life around us, it was like living in a fairy-tale. We would go to Casa Lebbes, a little jewelshop at number 1 Trincomalee Street in Kandy, and look at his jewels. He would pull out a soft leather bundle, undo it, and put before our eyes coloured wonders of sapphires, blue and lovely yellow ones, and rubies and emeralds. Lawrence bought me six blue sapphires and a yellow one: they were round in order to make a brooch in the form of a flower. The yellow one was the centre and the blue petal-shaped ones formed a flower round it. Also he bought me a cinnamon stone and a little box of moonstones. The blue sapphire flower I have lost, as I have lost so many things in my life, and the moonstones have disappeared, only the cinnamon stone remains. I wanted to go to Australia; it attracted me. Off we set again, trunks, Sicilian cart, and all, and went to Perth. Only Englishmen and Australians on the boat and it really felt as if one was going to the end of the earth.

We stayed only a little while near Perth and went a long way into that strange vague bush, everything so vague and dim, as before the days of creation. It wasn't born yet. Vague, remote, and unborn it made one feel oneself. There we stayed with Miss Skinner, whose manuscript Lawrence was looking over: "The Boy in the Bush." Later on, as I look back, it's all vague to me. Then, after a few weeks, we went on to Sydney.

We arrived in Sydney harbour—nice it was not knowing a soul.

A young officer on the boat had told me: "The rain on the tin roofs over the trenches always made me think of home." Sydney!

And there they were, the tin roofs of Sydney and the beautiful harbour and the lovely Pacific Coast, the air so new and clean. We stayed a day or two in Sydney, two lonely birds resting a little. And then we took a train with all our trunks and said: "We'll look out of the window and where it looks nice we'll get out." It looked very attractive along the coast but also depressing. We were passing deserted homesteads: both in America and Australia, these human abandoned efforts make one very sad. Then we came to Thirroul, we got out at four and by six o'clock we were settled in a beautiful bungalow right on the sea. Lined with jarra the rooms were, and there were great tanks for rain water and a stretch of grass going right down to the Pacific, melting away into a pale-blue and lucid, delicately tinted sky.

But what a state the bungalow was in! A family of twelve children had stayed there before us: beds and dusty rugs all over the place, torn sailing canvases on the porches, paper all over the garden, the beautiful jarra floors grey with dust and sand, the carpet with no colour at all, just a mess, a sordid mess the whole thing. So we set to and cleaned, cleaned and cleaned as we had done so many times before in our many temporary homes! Floors polished, the carpet taken in the garden and scrubbed, the torn canvases removed. But the paper in the garden was the worst; for days and days we kept gathering paper.

But I was happy: only Lawrence and I in this world. He always made a great big world for me, he gave it me whenever it was possible; whenever there was wonder left, we took it, and revelled in it.

The mornings, those sunrises over the Pacific had all the wonder of newness, of an uncreated world. Lawrence began to write "Kangaroo" and the days slipped by like dreams, but real as dreams are when they come true. The everyday life was so easy, the food brought to the house, especially the fish cart was a thrill: it let down a flap at the back and like pearls and jewels inside the cart lay the shiny fishes, all colours, all shapes, and we had to try them all.

We took long walks along the coast, lonely and remote and unborn. The weather was mild and full of life, we never got tired of the shore, finding shells for hours that the Pacific had rolled gently on to the sand.

Lawrence religiously read the "Sydney Bulletin." He loved it for all its stories of wild animals and people's living experiences. The only papers Lawrence ever read were the "Corriere della Sera," in the past, and the "Sydney Bulletin." I wonder whether this latter has retained the same character it had then; I haven't seen it since that time. It was our only mental food during that time.

I remember being amazed at the generosity of the people at the farms where we got butter, milk, and eggs: you asked for a pound of butter and you were given a big chunk that was nearly two pounds; you asked for two pints of milk and they gave you three; everything was lavish, like the sky and the sea and the land. We had no human contacts all these months: a strange experience: nobody bothered about us, I think.

At the library, strangely enough, in that little library of Thirroul we found several editions of Lawrence's condemned "Rainbow." We bought a copy—the librarian never knew that it was Lawrence's own book. Australia is like the "Hinterland der Seele."

Like a fantasy seemed the Pacific, pellucid and radiant, melting into the sky, so fresh and new always; then this primal radiance was gone one day and another primeval sea appeared. A storm was throwing the waves high into the air, they rose on the abrupt shore, high as in an enormous window. I could see strange sea-creatures thrown up from the deep: sword-fish and fantastic phenomena of undreamt deep-sea beasts I saw in those waves, frightening and never to be forgotten.

And then driving out of the tidy little town into the bush with the little pony cart. Into golden woods of mimosa we drove, or wattle, as the Australians call it. Mostly red flowers and yellow mimosa, many varieties, red and gold, met the eye, strange fern-trees, delicately leaved. We came to a wide river and followed it. It became a wide waterfall and then it disappeared into the earth. Disappeared and left us gaping. Why should it have disappeared, where had it gone?

Lawrence went on with "Kangaroo" and wove his deep underneath impressions of Australia into this novel. Thirroul itself was a new little bungalow town and the most elegant thing in it was a German gun that glistened steely and out of place there near the Pacific.

I would have liked to stay in Australia and lose myself, as it were, in this unborn country but Lawrence wanted to go to America. Mabel Dodge had written us that Lawrence must come to Taos in New Mexico, that he must know the Pueblo Indians, that the Indians say that the heart of the world beats there in New Mexico.

This gave us a definite aim and we began to get ready for America, in a few weeks.

DARLINGTON
WEST AUSTRALIA
15 MAY 1922

My dear Mother-in-Law:

So the new Jews must wander on. Frieda is very disappointed. She had hoped to find a new England or new Germany here, with much space and gayer people.

The land is here, sky high and blue and new as if you'd never taken a breath out of it: and the air is new, new, strong, fresh as silver. And the country is terribly big and empty, still uninhabited. The bush is grey and without end. No noise—quiet—and the white trunks of the gum-trees, all a little burnt: a wood and a prewood, not a jungle: something like a dream, a twilight wood that has not seen the day yet. It needs hundreds of years before it can live. This is the land where the unborn souls, strange and unknown, that will be born in five hundred years, live. A grey, strange spirit, and the people that are here are not really here: only like ducks that swim on the surface of a lake. But the country has a fourth dimension and the white people float like shadows on the surface. And they are not new people: very nervous, neurotic, they don't sleep well, as if they always felt a ghost near. I say, a new country is like sharp wine in which floats like a pearl the soul of an incoming people, till this soul is melted or dissolved. But this is stupid.

Thursday we go on by the P. & O. boat "Malwa" to Adelaide, Melbourne, and Sydney. We stay at Adelaide a day, sleep a night at Melbourne, and arrive at Sydney on the twenty-

seventh: nine days from Fremantle. That will be interesting. We have our tickets from Colombo to Sydney. It does please me to go on further. I think from Sydney we may go on to San Francisco, and stay a few weeks at Tahiti. And so round the world.

Oh, mother-in-law, it must be so! It is my destiny, this wandering. But the world is round and will bring us back to Baden.

Be well.

D. H. L.

(Translated from the German)

"WYEWURK"
THIRROUL
NEW SOUTH WALES
AUSTRALIA
28 MAY 1922

Meine liebe Schwiegermutter:

Diesmal schreibe dir auf Englisch, ich muss schnell sein. We got to Sydney on Saturday, after a fine journey. I like the P. & O. boats, with the dark servants. But that was a frightful wreck of the "Egypt" in the Bay of Biscay. We heard of it in Adelaide. Our captain of the "Malwa" changed from the "Egypt" only this very voyage. He was very upset—so was everybody. They say the Lascar servants are so bad in a wreck—rushing for the boats. But I don't believe all *of it.*

Anyway, here we are safe and sound. Sydney is a great fine town, half like London, half like America. The harbour is wonderful—a narrow gateway between two cliffs—then one sails through and is in another little sea, with many bays and gulfs. The big ferry steamers go all the time threading across the blue water, and hundreds of people always travelling.

But Sydney town costs too much, so we came down into the country. We are about fifty kilometres south of Sydney, on the coast. We have got a lovely little house on the edge of the low cliff just above the Pacific Ocean.—Der grosse oder stille Ozean, says Frieda. But it is by no means still. The heavy waves break with a great roar all the time: and it is so near. We have only our little grassy garden—then the low cliff—and then the great white rollers breaking, and the surf seeming to rush right under our feet as we sit at table. Here it is winter, but not cold. But today the sky is dark, and it makes me think of Cornwall. We have a coal fire going, and are very comfortable. Things go so quietly in Australia. It will not cost much to live here, food is quite cheap. Good meat is only fivepence or sixpence a pound—50 Pfg. ein Pfund.

But it is a queer, grey, sad country—empty, and as if it would never be filled. Miles and miles of bush—forlorn and lost. It all feels like that. Yet Sydney is a huge modern city.

I don't really like it, it is so raw—so crude. The people are so crude in their feelings—and they only want to be up-to-date in the "conveniences"—electric light and tramways and things like that. The aristocracy are the people who own big shops—and there is no respect for anything else. The working people very discontented—always threaten more strikes—always more socialism.

I shall cable to America for money, and sail in July across the Pacific to San Francisco—via Wellington, New Zealand, Raratonga, Tahiti, Honolulu—then to our Taos. And that is the way home—coming back. Next spring we will come to Germany. I've got a Heimweh for Europe: Sicily, England, Germany.

Auf Wiedersehen.

D. H. L.

I must hurry to catch the mail which leaves here tonight—leaves Sydney tomorrow, for Europe. Write to me:

care of Robert Mountsier
417 West 118 Street
New York City

I shall get your letters in America. Frieda ist so glücklich mit ihrem neuen Haus—macht alles so schön.

D. H. L.

THIRROUL, N.S.W.
AUSTRALIA
9 JUNE 1922

My dear Mother-in-Law:

We had two letters today—Anita's wedding letter, also the news that Nusch wants to leave Max. Oh, God! Revolution and earthquake! From your letters you seem to be a little angry. Are you angry that we wandered farther away, we wandering Jews? I tell you again, the world is round and brings the rolling stone home again. And I must go on till I find something that gives me peace. Last year I found it at Ebersteinburg. There I finished "Aaron's Rod" and my "Fantasia of the Unconscious." And now "Aaron" has appeared and this month the "Fantasia" will appear in New York. And I, I am in Australia, and suddenly I write again, a mad novel of Australia. That's how it goes. I hope I can finish it by August. Then, mother-in-law, again to the sea. We want to take the ship "Tahiti," that leaves Sydney on the tenth of August, and arrives on the sixteenth in Wellington, New Zealand; then to Raratonga and Papeete, capital of Tahiti, in the middle of the Pacific Ocean, and then, September fourth, we arrive at San Francisco, California. From San Francisco to Taos, New Mexico. And I believe, in the spring, you will see us again in Baden-Baden. I've only just enough money to take us to Taos. And then nothing. But it always comes.

It is nice here. You'd like this house very much: the large room with open fireplace and beautiful windows with red cur-

tains, and large verandas, and the grass and the sea, always big and noisy at our feet. We bathe at midday when the sun is very hot and the shores quite lonely, quite, quite lonely. Only the waves. The village is new and crude. The streets are not built, it is all sand and loam. It's interesting. The people are all very kind and yet strange to me. Postman and newspaper boy come riding on horses and whistle on a policeman's whistle when they have thrown in the letters or newspaper.

Meat is so cheap. Two good sheep's tongues ten cents, and a huge piece of beef enough for twelve people forty cents. We also have lovely fruit—apples, pears, passion-fruit, persimmons—and marvellous butter and milk.

And heaven and earth so new as if no man had ever breathed in it, no foot ever trodden on it. The great weight of the spirit that lies so heavily on Europe doesn't exist here. You feel a little like a child that has no real cares. It is interesting—a new experience.

It is your birthday in a little while. I send you a few cents, you can still have teas with old women. Greet all. Poor Else! I'm writing to her.

Leb wohl,

D. H. L.

(Translated from the German)

"WYEWURK"
THIRROUL
SOUTH COAST, N.S.W.
AUSTRALIA
13 JUNE 1922

Dear Else:

I have been wanting to write to you. The Schwiegermutter says that Friedel is ill with jaundice. I am so sorry, and do hope it is better by now.

I often think of you here, and wonder what you would think of this. We're in a very nice place: have got a delightful bungalow here about forty miles south of Sydney, right on the shore. We live mostly with the sea—not much with the land—and not at all with the people. I don't present any letters of introduction, we don't know a soul on this side of the continent: which is almost a triumph in itself. For the first time in my life I feel how lovely it is to know nobody in the whole country: and nobody can come to the door, except the tradesmen who bring the bread and meat and so on, and who are very unobtrusive. One nice thing about these countries is that nobody asks questions. I suppose there have been too many questionable people here in the past. But it's nice not to have to start explaining oneself, as one does in Italy.

The people here are awfully nice, casually: thank heaven I need go no further. The township is just a scatter of bungalows, mostly of wood with corrugated iron roofs, and with some quite good shops: "stores." It lies back from the sea. Nobody wants to be too near the sea here: only we are on the brink. About two miles inland there is a great long hill like a wall, facing the sea and running all down the coast. This is dark greyish with gum-trees, and it has little coal-mines worked into it. The men are mostly coal-miners, so I feel quite at home. The township itself —they never say village here—is all haphazard and new, the streets unpaved, the church built of wood. That part is pleasant —the newness. It feels so free. And though it is midwinter, and the shortest day next week, still every day is as sunny as our own summer, and the sun is almost as hot as our June. But the nights are cold.

Australia is a weird, big country. It feels so empty and untrodden. The minute the night begins to go down, even the towns, even Sydney, which is huge, begins to feel unreal, as if it were only a daytime imagination, and in the night it did not exist. That is a queer sensation: as if life here really had never entered *in: as if it were just sprinkled over, and the land lay untouched. They are terribly afraid of the Japanese. Practically all Australians, and especially Sydney, feel that once there was a fall in England, so that the Powers could not interfere, Japan would at once walk in and occupy the place. They seriously believe this: say it is even the most obvious thing for Japan to do, as a business proposition. Of course Australia would never be able to defend herself. It is queer to find these bogies wherever one goes. But I suppose they* may *materialize.*

Labour is very strong and very stupid. Everything except meat is exorbitantly expensive, many things twice as much as in England. And Australian apples are just as cheap in London as in Australia, and sometimes cheaper. It is all very irritating.

This is the most democratic place I have ever *been in. And the more I see of democracy the more I dislike it. It just brings everything down to the mere vulgar level of wages and prices, electric light and water closets, and nothing else. You* never *knew anything so nothing, nichts, nullus, niente, as the life here. They have good wages, they wear smart boots, and the girls all have silk stockings; they fly around on ponies and in buggies—sort of low one-horse traps—and in motorcars. They are always vaguely and meaninglessly on the go. And it all seems so empty, so* nothing, *it almost makes you sick. They are healthy, and to my thinking almost imbecile. That's what the life in a new country does to you: it makes you so material, so* outward, *that your real inner life and your inner self dies out, and you clatter round like so many mechanical animals. It is very like the Wells story—the fantastic stories. I feel if I lived in Australia for ever I should never open my mouth once to say one word that meant anything. Yet they are very trustful and kind and quite competent in their jobs. There's no need to lock your doors, nobody will come and steal. All the outside life is so* easy. *But there it ends. There's nothing else. The best society in the country are the shopkeepers—nobody is any better than anybody else, and it really* is *democratic. But it all feels so slovenly, slipshod, rootless, and empty, it is like a kind of dream. Yet the weird, unawakened country is wonderful and if one could have a dozen people, perhaps, and a big piece of land of one's own— But there, one can't.*

There is this for it, that here one doesn't feel the depression and the tension of Europe. Everything is happy-go-lucky, and one couldn't fret *about anything if one tried. One just doesn't care. And they are all like that.* Au fond *they don't care a straw about anything: except just their little egos. Nothing* really *matters. But they let the* little *things matter sufficiently to keep the whole show going. In a way it's a relief—a relief from the moral and mental and nervous tension of Europe. But to say the least, it's surprising. I never felt such a foreigner to any people in all my life as I do to these. An absolute foreigner, and I haven't one single thing to say to them.*

But I am busy doing a novel: with Australia for the setting: a queer show. It goes fairly quickly, so I hope to have it done by August. Then we shall sail via New Zealand and Tahiti for San Francisco, and probably spend the winter in Taos, New Mexico. That is what I think I want to do. Then the next spring come to Europe again. I feel I shall wander for the rest of my days. But I don't care.

I must say this new country has been a surprise to me. Flinders Petrie says new countries are no younger than their parent country. But they are older, more empty, and more devoid of religion or anything that makes for "quality" in life.

I have got a copy of "Aaron's Rod" for you, but am not sure whether I may post it from here or not. Trade relations with Germany don't start till August.

Write to me care of Robert Mountsier, 417 West 118th Street, New York. I wish I had good news for you. Frieda sleeps after her bath.

D. H. LAWRENCE

If a girl called Ruth Wheelock sends you a little note I gave her to introduce her to you, I think you'd like her. American, was in the consulate in Palermo—we knew her there and in Rome—both like her.

D. H. L.

She's not got any money, unless she earns some or her father gives her some.

We sailed from Sydney for San Francisco. It was a smallish boat with a stout jolly captain. We passed Raratonga and went on to Tahiti, always in perfect weather in the Pacific. Nothing but flying fish, porpoises, sky, the great sea, and our boat. Then Tahiti. It must have been so marvellous in the past, those gentle, too gentle handsome natives, with their huts, the perfection of the island in itself. But the joy of it was gone. The charming native women, who offered me old beads and flowers made me sad in their clumsy Mother Hubbard garments. I know how European diseases were wiping the natives out, the contact with Europe fatal to them. In the evening we saw a cinema in a huge kind of barn; there was a native king, enormous; he was in a box near the stage with several handsome wives. We had travelled with a cinema crowd from Tahiti. Near our cabin two of the young stars had their cabin. They seemed to sleep all day and looked white and tired in the evening. Cases of empty champagne bottles stood outside their cabin in the morning. One of them I had seen flirt quite openly with a passenger but when we arrived in San Francisco I saw her trip so innocently into the arms of a young man who was waiting for her. I remember in San Francisco how the moon at night made such a poor show above all the lights of the town.

We went into a cafeteria and did not know how to behave; how to take our plates and food.

America

We travelled from San Francisco to Taos in great expectation. It was September and the journey through the inner American desert very hot. We got out at Lamy to be met by Mabel Dodge who had brought us here. And as we looked out we saw Mabel standing there in a turquoise blue dress with much of the silver-and-turquoise Indian jewellery and by her side a handsome Indian in a blanket with a large silver belt going across his chest. I looked at Mabel. "She has eyes one can trust," I said to myself. And afterwards I always kept to this: people are what they are, whatever they may occasionally do.

When we came to Santa Fe all the hotels were full, so Mabel asked Witter Bynner to take us in. He did: us, the trunks, Sicilian cart and all.

The next morning we drove up through the vast wonderful desert country, with its clear pure air, driving through the Rio Grande canyon deep down by the river and then coming up on to the Taos plateau. Coming out of the canyon to the mesa is an unforgettable experience, with all the deep mountains sitting mysteriously around in a ring, and so much sky.

Mabel had prepared us a house all to ourselves in her "Mabel-town." The house stood on Indian land and belonged to Tony. It was a charming adobe house, with Mexican blankets and Indian paintings of Indian dances and animals, clean and full of sun.

A new life for us—and we began it straightaway. Out from

the pueblo to the east of us, a few miles away, came the feel of the Indians, so different from anything we had ever known. We neither of us wanted to stunt about it, but we were very happy. Tony went for two days with Lawrence to the Navajo country. I spent the days with Mabel and her friend Alice Corbin.

They asked me many questions, which I answered truthfully, giving the show away completely as usual. Then Mabel, with her great energy, took us all over the country: we saw the pueblo, we bathed in a hot radium spring by the Rio Grande. Mabel and Lawrence wanted to write a book together: about Mabel, it was going to be. I did not want this. I had always regarded Lawrence's genius as given to me. I felt deeply responsible for what he wrote. And there was a fight between us, Mabel and myself: I think it was a fair fight. One day Mabel came over and told me she didn't think I was the right woman for Lawrence and other things equally upsetting and I was thoroughly roused and said: "Try it then yourself, living with a genius, see what it is like and how easy it is, take him if you can."

And I was miserable thinking that Lawrence had given her a right to talk like this to me. When Lawrence came in, he saw that I was unhappy, and somebody had told him that Mabel's son John Evans had said: "My mother is tired of those Lawrences who sponge on her." This may have been pure malice, but Lawrence was in a fury too; not for nothing was his beard red; and he said: "I will pay the rent of the house and I'll leave as soon as I can."

And then he would draw me in a flood of tenderness and love and we would be washed clean of all our apartness and be together again. And Lawrence would rave against Mabel as only he could rave. When I wanted to stick up for her I would get it: "All women are alike, bossy, without any decency; it's your business to see that other women don't come too close to me."

That's what he said. It was all very well, but I didn't know how to do it.

We had learned to ride: a long thin Don Quixote of a Mexican had taught us how in a few rides across the open desert. I was terribly happy, feeling the live horse under me. Later on, Azul, my horse, would go like the wind with me and he seemed always aware of me when I was a bit scared.

So we left Mabel's ambient and went to live at the Del Monte Ranch, under the mountains. We had a log house, and the Hawks lived at the big house and in the lower log cabin lived two Danish painters who had come to stay with us; they had come from New York in the most trying old Lizzie that ever went along the road.

She coughed and trembled at the tiniest hill, she stuck and had to be shoved: she was a trial.

It was a real mountain winter. So sharp, knifey cold at night; snow and ice, and the Danes and Lawrence had to chop lots of wood.

We rode into the Lobo Canyon over the logs under the trees and one had to look out for one's head and knees when the horses tore along under the trees. Lawrence would say later on: "If you were only as nice with me as you are with Azul."

The friendship and fight with Mabel went on, off and on. She was so admirable in her terrific energy, in her resources and intelligence, but we couldn't get on, somehow.

I remember riding along in the car, when Lawrence said to

her: "Frieda is the freest human being I know." And I said to him, afterwards: "You needn't say nice things about me, just to make other people mad."

Tony would sing his Indian songs when driving. I had told him: "In our country, Tony, one crow means bad luck and two good luck." So he would watch for crows and say: "Two crows, Frieda."

///

In the spring we went to Mexico with Witter Bynner and Spud Johnson. After the hard winter, I clamoured for a first-rate hotel in Mexico City. But it wasn't a success, the first-rate hotel, after all, it seemed dull and a bit unclean; the ladies were so very painted and the men not attractive.

The journey across the lonely desert had been strange. The stations were only a few miserable houses and a big water tank and fine dust blew in at the window of the car, filling one's eyes and ears and nose, all one's pores with very fine sand.

Mexico City seemed like a would-be smart and grand lady to me, but she hadn't quite brought it off. The shabby parts were the most interesting. The Volador Market and all the fascinating baskets and ropes and saddles and belts, pots and dishes and leather-jackets.

One day we were in the cathedral plaza of Mexico City, Bynner and Spud and I, when on the top of the church we saw a red flag being hoisted. A crowd collected, soldiers appeared. Bynner and Spud had dashed into the dark hole of the door of the church tower. It was crowding with people. I stayed in the plaza, watching the tower on which were Bynner and Spud, fearing for their fate. My relief when they appeared after an hour was great.

In the Museum we saw among the Aztec relics coiled snakes

and other terrifying stone carvings, Maximilian's state carriage. That took me back to my childhood. One of the impressive figures of my childhood had been a Graf Geldern, long, lean, sad, and loosely built like a Mexican, in the uniform of a colonel of the "Totenkopfhusaren." He had been to Mexico with Maximilian. How he afterwards took Prussian service I don't know. When they shot Maximilian, they played "La Paloma." He had asked for it.

Lawrence went to Guadalajara and found a house with a patio on the Lake of Chapala. There Lawrence began to write his "Plumed Serpent." He sat by the lake under a pepper tree writing it. The lake was curious with its white water. My enthusiasm for bathing in it faded considerably when one morning a huge snake rose yards high, it seemed to me, only a few feet away. At the end of the patio we had the family that Lawrence describes in the "Plumed Serpent," and all the life of Chapala. I tried my one attempt at civilizing those Mexican children, but when they asked me one day: "Do you have lice too, Niña," I had enough and gave up in a rage. At night I was frightened of bandits and we had one of the sons of the cook sleeping outside our bedroom door with a loaded revolver, but he snored so fiercely that I wasn't sure whether the fear of bandits wasn't preferable. We quite sank into the patio life. Bynner and Spud came every afternoon, and I remember Bynner saying to me one day, while he was mixing a cocktail: "If you and Lawrence quarrel, why don't you hit first?" I took the advice and the next time Lawrence was cross, I rose to the occasion and got out of my Mexican indifference and flew at him.

All that time in Mexico seems to me, now, as if I had dreamt it, dreamt it intensely.

We went across the pale Lake of Chapala to a native village where they made serapes; they dyed the wool and wove them on simple looms. Lawrence made some designs and had them woven, as in the "Plumed Serpent."

Lawrence could only write in places where one's imagination could have space and free play, where the door was not closed to the future, where one's vision could people it with new souls to be born, who would live a new life.

I remember the Pyramids at Teotihuacan, that we saw with Spud and Bynner, I hanging around behind. It was getting dusky and suddenly I came on a huge stone snake, coiling green with great turquoise eyes, round the foot of a temple. I ran after the others for all I was worth.

I got a glimpse of old Mexico then, the old sacrifices, hearts still quivering held up to the sun, for the sun to drink the blood: there it had all happened, on the pyramid of the Sun.

And that awful goddess, who, instead of a Raphael bambino, brings forth an obsidian knife. Fear of these people who don't mind killing and don't mind dying. And I had seen a huge black Christ, in a church, with a black beard and long woman's hair and he wore little white, frilly knickers. Death and sacrifice and cruel gods seemed to reign in Mexico under its sunshine and splendour of flowers and lots of birds and fruit and white volcano peaks.

We went into a huge old Noah's Ark of a boat, called "Esmeralda," on the Lake of Chapala, with two other friends and Spud. Three Mexicans looked after the boat. They had guitars and sang their melancholy or fierce songs at the end of the boat. In the evening we slowly drifted along the large lake, that was more like a white sea, and, one day, we had no more to eat. So we landed on the island of the scorpions, still crowned by a Mexican empty prison, and only fit for scorpions. There Lawrence bought a live goat, but when we had seen our Mexican boatmen practically tearing the poor beast to pieces, our appetites vanished and we did not want to eat any more.

Lawrence's visions which he wrote in the "Plumed Serpent" seem so interwoven with everyday life. The everyday and the vision running on together day by day. That autumn we returned to America and spent some time in New Jersey. Lawrence remained in America and went again to Mexico. I went to Europe.

⁂

So I went to England alone and had a little flat in Hampstead to see something of my children. It was winter and I wasn't a bit happy alone there and Lawrence was always cross when I had this longing for the children upon me; but there it was, though now I know he was right: they didn't want me any more, they were living their own lives. I felt lost without him. Finally he came and wrote this cross and unjust letter to my mother:

Hotel Garcia
Guadalajara
Jalisco, Mexico
10 November 1923

My dear Mother-in-Law:

I had the two letters from Frieda at Baden, with the billet-doux from you. Yes, mother-in-law, I believe one has to be seventy before one is full of courage. The young are always half-hearted. Frieda also makes a long, sad nose and says she is writing to the moon—Guadalajara is no moon-town, and I am completely on the earth, with solid feet.

But I am coming back, am only waiting for a ship. I shall be in England in December. And in the spring, when the primroses are out, I shall be in Baden. Time goes by faster and faster. Frieda sent me Hartmann von Richthofen's letter. It was nice. But the women have more courage these days than the men—also a letter from Nusch, a little sad but lively. I hope to see her also in the spring. One must spit on one's hands and take firm hold. Don't you think so?

I was at the Barranca, a big, big ravine, and bathed in the hot springs—came home and found the whole of Germany in my room.

I like it here. I don't know how, but it gives me strength, this black country. It is full of man's strength, perhaps not woman's strength, but it is good, like the old German beer-for-the-heroes, for me. Oh, mother-in-law, you are nice and old, and understand, as the first maiden understood, that a man must be more than nice and good, and that heroes are worth more than saints. Frieda doesn't understand that a man must be a hero these days and not only a husband: husband also but more. I must go up and down through the world, I must balance Germany against Mexico and Mexico against Germany. I do not come for peace. The devil, the holy devil, has peace round his neck. I know it well, the courageous old one understands me better than the young one, or at least something in me she understands better. Frieda must always think and write and say and ponder how *she loves me. It is stupid. I am no Jesus that lies on his mother's lap. I go my way through the world, and if Frieda finds it such hard work to love me, then, dear God, let her love rest, give it holidays. Oh, mother-in-law, you understand, as my mother finally understood, that a man doesn't want, doesn't ask for love from his wife, but for strength, strength, strength. To fight, to fight, to fight, and to fight again. And one needs courage and strength and weapons. And the stupid woman keeps on saying love, love, love, and writes of love. To the devil with love! Give me strength, battle-strength, weapon-strength, fighting-strength, give me this, you woman!*

England is so quiet: writes Frieda. Shame on you that you ask for peace today. I don't want peace. I go around the world fighting. Pfui! Pfui! In the grave I find my peace. First let me fight and win through. Yes, yes, mother-in-law, make me an oak-wreath and bring the town music under the window, when the half-hero returns.

D. H. L.

(Translated from the German)

But I think he was right; I should have gone to meet him in Mexico, he should not have come to Europe; these are the mistakes we make, sometimes irreparable.

Finally he came and I was glad. Just before Christmas he came and we had some parties and saw some friends, but we wanted to go back to America in the spring and live at the ranch that Mabel Luhan had given me. She had taken me to the little ranch near Taos and I said: "This is the loveliest place I have ever seen." And she told me: "I give it you." But Lawrence said: "We can't accept such a present from anybody." I had a letter from my sister that very morning telling me she had sent the manuscript of "Sons and Lovers," so I told Lawrence: "I will give Mabel the MS. for the ranch." So I did.

Murry was coming to America too. First we went to Paris, where we stayed as in our own home at the Hôtel de Versailles.

Lawrence wanted me to have some new clothes. Mabel Harrison, who had a large studio opposite the hotel, told us of a good tailor nearby. Lawrence went with me. The stout little tailor draped himself with the cape we bought to show me how to wear it. "Voyez-vous, la ligne, Madame." He made me some other clothes and Lawrence remarked with wonder: "How is it possible that a man can throw all his enthusiasm into clothes for women?"

We went to Strassburg and Baden-Baden, a strange journey for me, going through French territory that had been German just a few years ago.

In the spring we went to America again and Dorothy Brett came with us. We only stayed a few days in New York and went on to Taos. We stayed with Mabel Luhan but, somehow, we didn't get on. I was longing to go to the ranch and live there. Lawrence was a bit afraid to tackle the forlorn little ranch. We had some ten or a dozen Indians to build up the tumble-down houses and corrals and everything. Then he loved it. We had to mend the irrigation ditch and we were impressed by the way Mr. Murry dragged huge pipes through the woods, just over no road, to the mouth of the Gallina Canyon of which we had the water rights. And I cooked huge meals for everybody. We all worked so hard. Brett, as everybody called her, straight from her studio life, was amazing for the hard work she would do. One day we cleaned our spring and carried huge stones until we nearly dropped. The spring is in a hollow, and I loved watching the horses play when they came to drink there, shoving each other's noses away from the water level and then tearing up the bank. We did it all ourselves for very little money for we didn't have much. We got a cow and had four horses: Azul, Aaron, and two others; and then we got chickens, all white ones, Leghorns. The beautiful cockerel was called Moses and Susan was the cow's name.

Lawrence got up at five o'clock each morning. With the opera glasses my mother had given him, he looked for Susan, who was an independent creature and loved to hide in the woods. There he would stand, when at last he had found her, and shake his forefinger at her—to my delight—and scold her, the black cow.

I made our own butter in a little glass churn and the chickens flourished on the buttermilk, and so did we in this healthy life. We made our own bread in the Indian oven outside, black bread and white and cakes, and Lawrence was terribly fussy about the bread, which had to be perfect. He made cupboards and chairs and painted doors and windows. He wrote and irrigated and it seems amazing that one single man got so much done. We rode and people stayed with us, and he was always there for everybody as if he did nothing at all. He helped Brett with her pictures and me with my poor attempts.

It was a wonderful summer; there were wild strawberries, that year, and back in the canyon raspberries as big as garden ones, but I was afraid to get them because I had heard that bears love raspberries. Bears won't do you any harm except when they have young. There were bears in the canyon—that seemed indeed the end of the world! The Brett had a tiny shanty in which she lived. She adored Lawrence and slaved for him.

In the autumn we went again to Mexico City. It was fun and we saw several people. In Mexico you could still feel a little lordly and an individual; Mexico has not yet been made "safe for democracy."

An amusing thing happened: Lawrence had become a member of the PEN Club and they gave an evening in his honour. It was a men's affair and he put on his black clothes and set off in the evening, and I, knowing how unused he was to public functions and how he really shrank from being a public figure, wondered in the hotel room how the evening would go off. Soon after ten o'clock he appeared.

"How was it?"

"Well, they read to me bits of 'The Plumed Serpent' in Spanish and I had to sit and listen and then they made a speech and I had to answer."

"What did you say?"

"I said: here we are together, some of us English, some Mexicans and Americans, writers and painters and business men and so on, but before all and above all we are *men* together tonight. That was about what I said. But a young Mexican jumped up: 'It's all very well for an Englishman to say I am a man first and foremost, but a Mexican cannot say so, he must be a Mexican above everything.' "

So we laughed, the only speech that Lawrence ever made falling so completely flat. They had missed the whole point, as so often.

Just as it was said of him that he wasn't patriotic; he who seemed to me England itself, a flower sprung out of its most delicate, courageous tradition, not the little bourgeois England but the old England of Palmerston, whom he admired, when men were still men and not mere social beings.

One day William Somerset Maugham was expected in Mexico City; so Lawrence wrote to him if they could meet. But Maugham's secretary answered for him, saying: "I hear we are going out to a friend's to lunch together who lives rather far out; let's share a taxi."

Lawrence was angry that Maugham had answered through his secretary and wrote back: "No, I won't share a car."

Brett came with us and she had a story from her sister, the Ranee of Sarawak, where Maugham had stayed and he and his secretary had nearly got drowned, shooting some rapids, I think. So there had been feeling there. And our hostess had a grudge against the secretary. Maugham sat next to me and I asked how he liked it here. He answered crossly: "Do you want me to admire men in big hats?"

I said: "I don't care what you admire." And then the lunch was drowned in acidity all around. But after lunch I felt sorry for Maugham: he seemed to me an unhappy and acid man, who got no fun out of living. He seemed to me to have fallen between two stools as so many writers do. He wanted to have his cake and eat it. He could not accept the narrow social world and yet he didn't believe in a wider human one. Commentators and critics of life and nothing more.

When I met other writers, then I knew without knowing how different altogether Lawrence was. They may have been good writers, but Lawrence was a genius.

The inevitability of what he elementally was and had to say at any price, his knowledge and vision, came to him from deeper secret sources than it is given to others to draw from. When I read Æschylus and Sophocles, then I know Lawrence is great, he is like these—greatest in his work, where human passions heave and sink and mingle and clash. The background of death is always there and the span of life is felt as fierce action. Life is life only when death is part of it. Not like the Christian conception that shuts death away from life and says death comes after: death is always there. I think the great gain of the war is a new reincorporation of death into our lives.

Then we went down to Oaxaca. We had again a house with a patio. There Lawrence wrote "Mornings in Mexico," with the parrots and Corasmin, the white dog, and the mozo. He rewrote and finished the "Plumed Serpent" there. There was malaria in Oaxaca, it had come with the soldiers, and the climate didn't suit him.

I went to the market with the mozo and one day he showed me in the square, in one of the bookshops, an undeniable caricature of Lawrence, and he watched my face to see how I would take it. I was thrilled! To find in this wild place, with its Zapotec and undiluted Mexican tribes, anything so civilized as a caricature of Lawrence was fun. I loved the market and it was only distressing to see the boy with his basket so utterly miserable at my paying without bargaining: it was real pain to him. But the lovely flowers and everything seemed so cheap.

Meanwhile Lawrence wrote at home and got run down. The Brett came every day and I thought she was becoming too much part of our lives and I resented it. So I told Lawrence: "I want the Brett to go away," and he raved at me, said I was a jealous fool. But I insisted and so Brett went up to Mexico City. Then Lawrence finished "The Plumed Serpent," already very ill, and later on he told me he wished he had finished it differently. Then he was very ill. I had a local native doctor who was scared at having anything to do with a foreigner and he didn't come. Lawrence was very ill, much more ill than I knew, fortunately. I can never say enough of the handful of English and Americans there: how good they were to us. Helping in every way. I thought these mine-owners and engineers led plucky and terrible lives. Always fever, typhoid, malaria, danger from bandits, never feeling a bit safe with their lives. And so I was amazed at the "Selbstverständlichkeit" with which they helped us. It was so much more than Christian, just natural: a fellow-Englishman in distress: let's help him. Lawrence himself thought he would die.

"You'll bury me in this cemetery here," he would say, grimly.

"No, no," I laughed, "it's such an ugly cemetery, don't you think of it."

And that night he said to me: "But if I die, nothing has mattered but you, nothing at all." I was almost scared to hear him say it, that, with all his genius, I should have mattered so much. It seemed incredible.

I got him better by putting hot sandbags on him, that seemed to comfort his tortured inside.

One day we had met a missionary and his wife, who lived right in the hills with the most uncivilized tribe of Indians. He didn't look like a missionary but like a soldier. He told me he had been an airman, and there far away in Oaxaca he told me how he was there when Manfred Richthofen was brought down behind the trenches and in the evening at mess one of the officers rose and said: "Let's drink to our noble and generous enemy."

For me to be told of this noble gesture made in that awful war was a great thing.

Then I remember the wife appeared with a very good bowl of soup when Lawrence was at his worst, and then prayed for him by his bedside in that big bare room. I was half afraid and wondered how Lawrence would feel. But he took it gently and I was half laughing, half crying over the soup and the prayer.

While he was so ill an earthquake happened into the bargain, a thunderstorm first, and the air made you gasp. I felt ill and feverish and Lawrence so ill in the next room—dogs howled and asses and horses and cats were scared in the night—and to my horror I saw the beams of my roof move in and out of their sheaves.

"Let's get under the bed if the roof falls!" I cried.

At last, slowly, slowly, he got a little better. I packed up to go to Mexico City. This was a crucifixion of a journey for me. We travelled through the tropics. Lawrence in the heat so weak and ill and then the night we stayed halfway to Mexico City in a hotel. There, after the great strain of his illness, something broke in me. "He will never be quite well again, he

LAWRENCE AND FRIEDA IN MEXICO

LAWRENCE IN MEXICO

is ill, he is doomed. All my love, all my strength, will never make him whole again." I cried like a maniac the whole night. And he disliked me for it. But we arrived in Mexico City. I had Dr. Uhlfelder come and see him. One morning I had gone out and when I came back the analyst doctor was there and said, rather brutally, when I came into Lawrence's room: "Mr. Lawrence has tuberculosis." And Lawrence looked at me with such unforgettable eyes.

"What will she say and feel?" And I said: "Now we know, we can tackle it. That's nothing. Lots of people have that." And he got slowly better and could go to lunch with friends. But they, the doctors, told me:

"Take him to the ranch; it's his only chance. He has T.B. in the third degree. A year or two at the most."

With this bitter knowledge in my heart I had to be cheerful and strong. Then we travelled back to the ranch and were tortured by immigration officials, who made all the difficulties in the ugliest fashion to prevent us from entering the States. If the American Embassy in Mexico hadn't helped we would not have been able to go to the ranch that was going to do Lawrence so much good.

Slowly at the ranch he got better. The high clear air, short sunbaths, our watching and care, and the spring brought life back into him. As he got better he began writing his play "David," lying outside his little room on the porch in the sun.

I think in that play he worked off his struggle for life. Old Saul and the young David—old Samuel's prayer is peculiarly moving in its hopeless love for Saul—so many different motifs, giant motifs, in that play.

Mabel took us to a cave along the road near Arroyo Seco and he used it for his story "The Woman Who Rode Away."

Brett was always with us. I liked her in many ways; she was so much her own self.

I said to her: "Brett, I'll give you half a crown if you contradict Lawrence," but she never did. Her blind adoration for him, her hero-worship for him was touching, but naturally it was balanced by a preconceived critical attitude towards me. He was perfect and I always wrong, in her eyes.

When the Brett came with us Lawrence said to me: "You know, it will be good for us to have the Brett with us, she will stand between us and people and the world." I did not really want her with us, and had a suspicion that she might not want to stand between us and the world, but between him and me. But no, I thought, I won't be so narrow-gutted, one of Lawrence's words, I will try.

So I looked after Brett and was grateful for her actual help. She did her share of the work. I yelled down her ear-trumpet, her Toby, when people were there, that she should not feel out of it. But as time went on she seemed always to be there, my privacy that I cherished so much was gone. Like the eye of the Lord, she was; when I washed, when I lay under a bush with a book, her eyes seemed to be there, only I hope the eye of the Lord looks on me more kindly. Then I detested her, poor Brett, when she seemed deaf and dumb and blind to everything quick and alive. Her adoration for Lawrence seemed a silly old habit. "Brett," I said, "I detest your adoration for Lawrence, only one thing I would detest more, and that is if you adored me."

When I finally told Lawrence in Oaxaca: "I don't want Brett such a part of our life, I just don't want her," he was cross at first, but then greatly relieved.

How thrilling it was to feel the inrush of new vitality in him;

it was like a living miracle. A wonder before one's eyes. How grateful he was inside him! "I can do things again. I can live and do as I like, no longer held down by the devouring illness." How he loved every minute of life at the ranch. The morning, the squirrels, every flower that came in its turn, the big trees, chopping the wood, the chickens, making bread, all our hard work, and the people and all assumed the radiance of new life.

He worked hard as a relaxation and wrote for hard work.

Palace Hotel
San Francisco, U.S.A.
5 September 1922

Dear Mother-in-Law:

We arrived yesterday, the journey good all the way. Now we sit in the Palace Hotel, the first hotel of San Francisco. It was first a hut with a corrugated iron roof, where the ox-wagons unhitched. Now a big building, with post and shops in it, like a small town in itself: is expensive, but for a day or two it doesn't matter. We were twenty-five days at sea and are still landsick—the floor ought to go up and down, the room ought to tremble from the engines, the water ought to swish around but doesn't, so one is landsick. The solid ground almost hurts. We have many ship's friends here, are still a jolly company.

I think we shall go to Taos Tuesday or Friday: two days by train, a thousand miles by car. We have such nice letters and telegrams from Mabel Dodge and Mountsier. Mabel says: "From San Francisco you are my guests, so I send you the railway tickets"—so American! Everybody is very nice. All is comfortable, comfortable, comfortable—I really hate this mechanical comfort.

I send you thirty dollars—I have no English cheques—till I arrive in Taos. I will send you English money, with the rise of the valuta. Does Else need any money? I don't know how much I've got, but our life in Taos will cost little—rent free and wood free. Keep well, mother-in-law. I wait for news from you.

D. H. L.

(Translated from the German)

Taos
New Mexico
U.S.A.
27 September 1922

My dear Else:

Well, here we are in the Land of the Free and the Home of the Brave. But both freedom and bravery need defining. The Eros book came, and I shall read it as soon as we get breathing space. Even though we are in the desert, in the sleepy land of the Mexican, we gasp on the breath of hurry.

We have got a very charming adobe house on the edge of the Indian Reservation—very smartly furnished with Indian village-made furniture and Mexican and Navajo rugs, and old European pottery.

Behind runs a brook—in front the desert, a level little plain all grey, white-grey sage brush, in yellow flower—and from this plain rise the first Rocky Mountains, heavy and solid. We are seven thousand feet above the sea—in a light, clear air.

The sun by day is hot, night is chilly. At the foot of the sacred Taos Mountain, three miles off, the Indians have their pueblo, like a pile of earth-colored cube-boxes in a heap: two piles rather, one on one side of the stream, one on the other. The stream waters the little valley, and they grow corn and maize, by irrigation. This pueblo owns four square miles of land. They are nearer the Aztec type of Indian—not like Apaches, whom I motored last week to see—far over these high, sage-brush deserts and through canyons.

These Indians are soft-spoken, pleasant enough—the young ones come to dance to the drum—very funny and strange. They are Catholics, but still keep the old religion, making the weather and shaping the year: all very secret and important to them. They are naturally secretive, and have their backs set against our form of civilization. Yet it rises against them. In the pueblo they have mowing machines and threshing machines, and American schools, and the young men no longer care so much for the sacred dances.

And after all, if we have to go ahead, we must ourselves go ahead. We can go back and pick up some threads—but these Indians are up against a dead wall, even more than we are: but a different wall.

Mabel Sterne is very nice to us—though I hate living on somebody else's property and accepting their kindnesses. She very much wants me to write about here. I don't know if I ever shall. Because though it is so open, so big, free, empty, and even aboriginal—still it has a sort of shutting-out quality, obstinate.

Everything in America goes by will. *A great negative* will *seems to be turned against all spontaneous life—there seems to be no* feeling *at all—no genuine bowels of compassion and sympathy: all this gripped, iron,* benevolent *will, which in the end is diabolic. How can one write about it, save analytically?*

Frieda, like you, always secretly hankered after America and its freedom: It's very freedom not *to feel. But now she is just beginning to taste the iron ugliness of what it means, to live by will* against *the spontaneous inner life, superimposing the individual, egoistic will over the real genuine sacred life. Of course I know you will jeer when I say there is any such thing as sacred spontaneous life, with its pride and its sacred power. I know you too believe in the screwed-up human will* dominating *life. But I don't. And that's why I think America is neither free nor brave, but a land of tight, iron-clanking little* wills, *everybody trying to put it over everybody else, and a land of men absolutely devoid of the real courage of trust, trust in life's sacred spontaneity. They can't trust life until they can* control *it. So much for them—cowards! You can have the Land of the Free—as much as I know of it. In the spring I want to come back to Europe.*

I send you ten pounds to spend for the children—since you suffer from the exchange. I hope in this little trifle you can profit by it. F. sends her love.

D. H. Lawrence

P.S. *If you want winter clothing, or underclothing, for the children or yourself or Alfred, write to my sister, Mrs. L. A. Clarke, Grosvenor Rd., Ripley near Derby—tell her just what you want, and she will send it. I shall pay her—I have told her you will write—so don't hesitate.*

DEL MONTE RANCH
QUESTA, NEW MEXICO
5 DECEMBER 1922

My dear Mother-in-Law:

You see, we have flown again, but not far—only twenty-five kilometres, and here we are in an old log-house with five rooms, very primitive, on this big ranch. Behind, the Rocky Mountains, pines and snow-peaks; around us the hills—pine trees, cedars, greasewood, and a small grey bush of the desert. Below, the desert, great and flat like a shadowy lake, very wide. And in the distance more mountains, with small patches of snow—and the sunsets! Now you see the picture.

The Hawk family live five minutes from here, then no houses for four kilometres. Behind, no house for three hundred kilometres or more. Few people, an empty, very beautiful country.

We have hewn down a great balsam pine and cut it to pieces—like a quarry—the gold wood.

We have for companions two young Danes, painters: they will go into a little three-room cabin nearby. Our nearest neighbour, Hawk, is a young man, thirty years old, has a hundred and fifty half-wild animals, a young wife, is nice, not rich.

You have asked about Mabel Dodge: American, rich, only child, from Buffalo on Lake Erie, bankers, forty-two years old, has had three husbands—one Evans (dead), one Dodge (divorced), and one Maurice Sterne (a Jew, Russian, painter, young, also divorced). Now she has an Indian, Tony, a stout chap. She has lived much in Europe—Paris, Nice, Florence—

is a little famous in New York and little loved, very intelligent as a woman, another "culture-carrier," likes to play the patroness, hates the white world and loves the Indian out of hate, is very "generous," wants to be "good" and is very wicked, has a terrible will-to-power, you know—she wants to be a witch and at the same time a Mary of Bethany at Jesus's feet—a big, white crow, a cooing raven of ill-omen, a little buffalo.

The people in America all want power, but a small, personal base power: bullying. They are all bullies.

Listen, Germany, America is the greatest bully the world has ever seen. Power is proud. But bullying is democratic and base.

Basta, we are still "friends" with Mabel. But do not take this snake to our bosom. You know, these people have only money, nothing else but money, and because all the world wants money, all the money, America has become strong, proud and over-powerful.

If one would only say: "America, your money is sh . . . , go and sh . . . more"—then America would be a nothing.

(Translated from the German)

HOTEL MONTE CARLO
URUGUAY, MEXICO
27 APRIL 1923

My dear Mother-in-Law:

We are still here, still making excursions. We can't make up our minds to go away. Tomorrow I go to Guadalajara and the Chapala Lake. There you have the Pacific breeze again, straight from the Pacific. One doesn't want to come back to Europe. All is stupid, evilly stupid and no end to it. You must be terribly tired of this German tragedy—all without meaning, without direction, idea, or spirit. Only money-greed and impudence. One can't do anything, nothing at all, except get bored and wicked. Here in Mexico there's also Bolshevism and Fascism and revolutions and all the rest of it. But I don't care. I don't listen. And the Indians remain outside. Revolutions come and revolutions go but they remain the same. They haven't the machinery of our consciousness, they are like black water, over which go our dirty motorboats, with stink and noise—the water gets a little dirty but does not really change.

I send you ten pounds and five for Else. I hope it arrives soon. A Hamburg-America boat goes every month from Vera Cruz to Hamburg. It must be lovely spring in Germany. If only men were not so stupid and evil, I would so love to be in Ebersteinburg when the chestnuts are in bloom. Have you seen "The Captain's Doll"? It ought to amuse you.

A thousand greetings.

D. H. L.

(Translated from the German)

ZARAGOZA 4
CHAPALA, JALISCO
MEXICO
31 MAY, CORPUS CHRISTI DAY

My dear Mother-in-Law:

You will think we are never coming back to Europe. But it isn't so.

But I always had the idea of writing a novel here in America. In the U. S. I could do nothing. But I think here it will go well. I have already written ten chapters and if the Lord helps me I shall have finished the first full sketch by the end of June. And then we will come home at once.

I must go by way of New York because of business and because it is shorter and cheaper. But in July New York is very hot, and the nastiest heat, they say. Still, we won't stay more than a fortnight, from there to England and from England to Germany—very likely in September: my birthday month that I like so much.

Today is Corpus Christi and they have a procession. But there are no lovely birches as in Ebersteinburg two years ago. They only carry little palms into the churches, and palms aren't beautiful like our trees, and this eternal sun is not as joyous as our sun. It is always shining and is a little mechanical.

But Mexico is very interesting: a foreign people. They are mostly pure Indians, dark like the people in Ceylon but much stronger. The men have the strongest backbones in the world, I believe. They are half civilized, half wild. If they only had a new faith they might be a new, young, beautiful people. But as Christians they don't get any further, are melancholy inside, live without hope, are suddenly wicked, and don't like to work. But they are also good, can be gentle and honest, are very quiet, and are not at all greedy for money, and to me that is marvellous, they care so little for possessions, here in America where the whites care for nothing else. But not the peon. He has not this fever to possess that is a real "Weltschmerz" with us.

And now you know where we are and how it is with us. I'll send you a beautiful serape—blanket—for your birthday.

Auf Wiedersehen.

D. H. Lawrence

(Translated from the German)

LAWRENCE IN MEXICO

CARE OF SELTZER
5 WEST 50TH STREET
NEW YORK CITY
7 AUGUST 1923

My dear Mother-in-Law:

We are still here in America—I find my soul doesn't want to come to Europe, it is like Balaam's ass and can't come any further. I am not coming, but Frieda is. Very likely she will come by the S.S. "Orbita," on the eighteenth, from New York, for Southampton, England. She will be in London on the twenty-fifth, stays there a fortnight, then to Baden. I remain on this side: go to California, Los Angeles, where we have friends, and if it is nice there, Frieda can come there in October. I don't know why I can't go to England. Such a deadness comes over me, if I only think of it, that I think it is better if I stay here, till my feeling has changed.

I don't like New York—a big, stupid town, without background, without a voice. But here in the country it is green and still. But I like Mexico better. With my heart I'd like to come—also with my feet and eyes. But my soul can't. Farewell. Later on, the ass will be able to come.

D. H. L.

(Translated from the German)

110 Heath Street
Hampstead, London, N.W.3
14 December 1923

My dear Mother-in-Law:

Here I am back again. Frieda is nice but England is ugly. I am like a wild beast in a cage—it is so dark and closed-in here and you can't breathe freely. But the people are friendly. Frieda has a nice apartment but I go about like an imprisoned coyote—can't rest.

I think we'll go to Paris at the end of the month and then Baden.

Do you hear me howl?

D. H. L.

(Translated from the German)

PARIS
HÔTEL DE VERSAILLES
60 BOULEVARD MONTPARNASSE
SATURDAY

Dearest Mütchen:

We are sitting in bed, have had our coffee, the clock says 8:30, and we see the people and the carriages pass on the boulevard outside in the morning sun. The old men and women shake their carpets on their balconies in the tall house opposite, cleaning hard. Paris is still Paris.

We went to Versailles yesterday. It is stupid, so very big and flat, much too big for the landscape. No, such hugeness is merely blown up frog, that wants to make himself larger than nature and naturally he goes pop! Le Roi Soleil was like that—a very artificial light. Frieda was terribly disappointed in Le Petit Trianon of Marie Antoinette—a doll's palace and a doll's Swiss village from the stage. Poor Marie Antoinette, she wanted to be so simple and become a peasant, with her toy Swiss village and her nice, a little ordinary, Austrian, blond face. Finally she became too simple, without a head.

On the great canal a few people skated, a very few people, little and cold and without fun, between those well-combed trees that stand there like hair with an elegant parting. And these are the great. Man is stupid. Naturally the frog goes pop!

Frieda has bought two hats and is proud of them.

Tomorrow we go to Chartres to see the cathedral. And that is our last outing. Tuesday we go to London.

Now, mother-in-law, you know all we are doing and can travel along with us. Such is life. We can go together in spite of separation and you can travel, travel in spite of old age.

Salutations, Madame,

D. H. L.

(Translated from the German)

DEL MONTE RANCH
QUESTA, NEW MEXICO
28 JUNE 1924

Dearest Mother-in-Law:

It's so long since I wrote you, but we had much to do here and my desire for writing is weak. I don't know why, but words and speech bore me a little. We know so well without saying anything. I know you, you know me, so I need no longer speak on paper.

You know, Frieda is quite proud of her ranch and her horse Azul, that's the one with two wives—my Poppy, who is very shy but beautiful, sorrel and quick, and then old Bessy, Brett's horse. Bessy is also red, or sorrel.

Every evening we go down to Del Monte, only three and a half kilometres, through woods and over the Lobo brook. You know, this place is called Lobo, which means "wolf" in Spanish.

Frieda is always talking to her Azul. "Yes, Azul, you're a good boy! Yes, my Azul, go on, go on, then! Yes! Are you afraid, silly horse! It's only a stone, a great white stone, why are you afraid then?" That's how she is always talking to him, because she is a little afraid herself.

There is always something to do here. I've written two stories. Right now we're building a roof over the little veranda before the kitchen door, with eight small pillars of pinewood and boards on top—very nice. It's nearly finished. You know, we've also got an Indian oven made of adobe. It stands outside, not far from the kitchen door, built like a beehive.

Last week came Francisca, the Indian servant at Del Monte. We baked bread and roasted chickens in the oven—very good. We can bake twenty loaves of bread in half an hour in it.

Five minutes' walk from here are the tents and beds of the Indians, still standing. Frieda and I slept there once, under the big stars that hang low on the mountains here. Morning comes and a beautiful grey squirrel runs up the balsam pine and scolds us. No one else in the world, only the great desert below, to the west. We don't go much to Taos and Mabel does not come often. We have our own life. The Brett is a little simple but harmless, and likes to help. Else writes Friedel is coming to America. He will likely come here. I think Else may also come, she has a desire for America. All right, but life in America is empty and stupid, more empty and stupid than with us. I mean the city and village life. But here, where one is alone with trees and mountains and chipmunks and desert, one gets something out of the air, something wild and untamed, cruel and proud, beautiful and sometimes evil—that is really America. But not the America of the whites.

Here comes your birthday again, you old Valkyrie, so you leap on the horse of your spirit from one year's peak to the next, and look always further into the future. I send you a cheque. How gladly would I be with you, to drink your health in good Moselle. Here there is no wine and the "prosit" cannot sound through the pines. But next year we will drink together to your birthday.

Auf Wiedersehen.

D. H. L.

FRIEDA LAWRENCE ON AZUL

P.S. I forgot, we have two small Bibble's-sons, two little dogs from our Pips. They are six weeks old, named Roland and Oliver, and are gay, small, and fat, and lift their paws like Chinese lions.

(Translated from the German)

SANTA FE
14 AUGUST 1924

[To Else]

We are motoring with Mabel Luhan to the Hopi country—hotter down here.

Curtis Brown wrote they were arranging with you for "Boy in the Bush"—hope everything is satisfactory, and what a pity Baltimore is so far.

D. H. L.

Del Monte Ranch
Questa, New Mexico
26 October 1924

Dear Mother-in-Law:

We are home again, thank God. When one has been for three days with people one has had enough, quite enough. But next week we are going away, to stay a few days in Taos, then on to Mexico. Write to me care of British Consulate, 1 Avenida Madero, Mexico, D. F., until I give you a new address.

The Brett will go with us: we do not know what else she could do, and she cannot remain here alone.

I am glad to go to Mexico. I don't know why, but I always want to travel south. It is already cold here, especially at night. The sun doesn't come over the hills till seven-thirty, then it turns warm and the horses stand stone-still, numbed by the cold, in the middle of the alfalfa field soaking themselves in the sun's heat. For the most the sun is hot like July but today there are clouds.

I hope you will get your parcel, with blanket and picture. You will like them, I'm sure. I send you ten pounds for wood, you must keep nice and warm.

Here we shut everything up. The better things—silverware, rugs, beds, pictures, we take down on the wagon to good William and Rachel. Del Monte belongs to Mr. Hawk, William's father. The parents have a biggish house but go to California a lot. The young ones, William and Rachel, are in the log-cabin where we stayed two years ago. They make butter there and look after the cows and chickens.

Every evening we ride down to get the milk and the post from William. He always brings the letters up from the post box. Rachel and William will take good care of our things. Monday, Mr. Murray, a workman, comes to put up the shutters. We shall leave the horses here till December when the big snow comes. Then William will take them to Del Monte, only two and a half kilometres away, and feed them every day with alfalfa till spring when we come back again.

I don't know how long we want to stay in Mexico City. I want to go southward to Oaxaca where the Mayas and Zapotec Indians live. It is always warm there, even hot. There I would like to finish my novel, "The Plumed Serpent."

Here the hills are golden with aspen and cottonwoods and red with scrub-oak, wonderful. The pines and firs nearly black. A lovely moment, a beautiful moment, but it will not last.

Auf Wiedersehen, mother-in-law. Winter comes again for old ladies, too bad.

D. H. L.

(Translated from the German)

[A letter to Lawrence from his mother-in-law]

Baden
Sunday 9 November 1924

My dear Fritzl:

Else has vanished in beautiful winter sunshine and I sit alone in my lonely wintry room. So far I got yesterday when the charwoman came and today, O jubilee, O triumph, came the cheque and the parcel. Like a demon I rushed to the station, number 2 brought the parcel, too heavy for me, and what came forth! Moved, admiring and happy, I sit and look. How you have painted! No, how adorable is the ranch! Here the stones speak! I understand that you love being there. I see it all—O dear son-in-law, how happy you have made me! I would like to pack up and come. If I were only younger! No, those horses and the lovely tree! But I think the winter is too cold—and I can smell those flowers, almost, so charming and gay and colourful. I called all the ladies in my tempestuous joy and all admired with me. What treasures—the blanket is just what I needed. The little original cover I put on my cane chair— My room looks quite Mexican! At once I will have the two pictures framed and hang them where I can see them— Now I know how you live, oh, the wonderful tree!

The tablecloth Else shall have for Christmas; the bag is ideal. All is spread out on the table before me and I do nothing but look and enjoy it all day! So much love in it all! I feel it so deeply and gratefully. May it shine into your own lives your thoughts of the old mother. I am looking forward to Else's coming back—how she will open her eyes.

I hope you are really comfortable somewhere and have good news of the horses and the ranch. The parcel has taken five weeks but all arrived safely. I hope you found my letters in Mexico. I can't thank you enough. I have not enjoyed anything so much for a long time and must always have another look at the cabin.

All luck to you—keep well.

With all my heart, your happy

MOTHER

(Translated from the German)

Del Monte Ranch
Questa, New Mexico
15 April 1925

My dear Mother-in-Law:

Today came your two letters. So you went up the Merkur. Yes, you are younger than I am.

We have been at the ranch a week already. We found all well and safe, nothing broken, nothing destroyed. Only the mice found Mabel's chair and ate the wool.

In the second house we have two young Indians, Trinidad and Rufina, husband and wife. Rufina is short and fat, waddles like a duck in high, white Indian boots—Trinidad is like a girl, with his two plaits. Both are nice, don't sweat over their work, but do what we want. We still have the three horses but they are down with the Hawks, till the alfalfa and the grass have grown a bit.

We had three cold days—the wind can come ice-cold. I had a cold again. But now the weather is mild and warm, very beautiful, and spring in the air. All was washed very clean on the land, coming out of a yard of snow. Now the first anemones have come, built like crocuses but bigger and prouder, hairy on the brown-red earth under the pines. But everything is very dry again, the grass has hardly appeared, and yet it won't grow any higher. We hoped for rain or snow again.

Brett stays down on Del Monte, in a little house by herself, near the old Hawks. She wanted to come up here but Frieda said no. And so we are only two whites and two reds, or rather yellow-browns, on the ranch. Trinidad fetches milk and butter and eggs from Del Monte. I lie in the sun. Frieda is happy to be on her ranch. Friedel comes in May—writes very happily, very likely he will return to the Fatherland at the end of the summer. For September we also think to come to England and Germany. But the Lord's will be done. We bought a buggy and Trinidad will be coachman. I don't work this year, am cross that I was so ill. Mabel is still in New York, but Friday Tony came.

Tomorrow Frieda goes to Taos by car. We are nice and warm here and have all one needs.

Well that you have friends with you. I send you a little pin-money.

Auf Wiedersehen.

D. H. L.

(Translated from the German)

THE LAWRENCES' RANCH ON THE LOBO,
SAN CRISTOBAL, N. M.

S.S. "Resolute"
25 September 1925

Meine liebe Schwiegermutter:

This is the second day at sea—very nice, with blue running water and a fresh wind. I am quite glad to be out of that America for a time: it's so tough and wearing, with the iron springs poking out through the padding.

We shall be in England in five more days—I think we shall take a house by the sea for a while, so Frieda can have her children to stay with her. And I must go to my sisters and see their new house. And then we must hurry off to Baden-Baden, before winter sets in.

I don't feel myself very American: no, I am still European. It seems a long time since we heard from you—I hope it's a nice autumn. In New York it was horrid, hot and sticky.

Save me a few good Schwarzwald apples, and a bottle of Kirschwasser, and a few leaves on the trees, and a few alten Damen in the Stift to call me Herr Doktor when I'm not one, and a hand at whist with you and my kurzröckige Schwägerin, and a Jubiläum in the Stiftsköniginkammer. The prodigal children come home, vom Schwein gibt's kein mehr, nur vom Kalb.

à bientôt!
auf baldige Wiedersehen!
hasta luego!
till I see you!

D. H. L.

Going Back to Europe

At the end of the summer he became restless again and wanted to go to Europe. To the Mediterranean he wished to go. So on the coast, not far from Genoa, we found Spotorno, that Martin Secker had told us was not overrun with foreigners. Under the ruined castle I saw a pink villa that had a friendly look and I wondered if we could have it. We found the peasant Giovanni who looked after it. Yes, he thought we could. It belonged to a Tenente dei Bersaglieri in Savona. We were staying at the little inn by the sea, when the bersaglieri asked for us. Lawrence went and returned. "You must come and look at him, he is so smart." So I went and found a figure in uniform with gay plumes and blue sash, as it was the Queen's birthday. We took the Bernarda and the tenente became a friend of ours. Lawrence taught him English on Sundays, but they never got very far.

My daughter Barbara, now grown up, was coming to stay with me. She was coming for the first time. I was beside myself with joy to have her. I had not waited in vain for so many years and longed for these children. But Lawrence did not share my joy. One day at our evening meal came the outburst: "Don't you imagine your mother loves you," he said to Barby; "she doesn't love anybody, look at her false face." And he flung half a glass of red wine in my face. Barby, who besides my mother and myself was the only one not to be scared of him, sprang up. "My mother is too good for you," she blazed at him, "much too good; it's like pearls thrown to the swine." Then we both began to cry. I went to my room offended.

"What happened after I went?" I asked Barby later on.

"I said to him: 'Do you care for her?' 'It's indecent to ask,' he answered; 'haven't I just helped her with her rotten painting?' " Which again puzzled me because he would gladly help anybody. It did not seem a sign of love to me. Then my daughter Else came too. But evidently to counterbalance my show Lawrence had asked his sister Ada and a friend to come and stay, so there were two hostile camps. Ada arrived and above me, in Lawrence's room with the balcony, I could hear him complaining to her about me. I could not hear the words but by the tone of their voices I knew.

His sister Ada felt he belonged to her and the past, the past with all its sad memories. Of course it had been necessary for him to get out of his past and I had, of equal necessity, to fight that past, though I liked Ada for herself.

Lawrence was ill with all this hostility. I was grieved for him. So one evening I went up to his room and he was so glad I came. I thought all was well between us. In the morning Ada and I had bitter words. "I hate you from the bottom of my heart," she told me. So another night I went up to Lawrence's room and found it locked and Ada had the key. It was the only time he had really hurt me; so I was quite still. "Now I don't care," I said to myself.

He went away with Ada and her friend, hoping at the last I would say some kind word, but I could not. Lawrence went to Capri to stay with the Brewsters.

But I was happy with the two children. The spring came with its almond blossoms and sprouting fig-trees. Barby rushed up the hills with her paint box, her long legs carrying her like a deer. We lay in the sun and I rejoiced in her youthful bloom. Then a picture arrived from Lawrence. There was Jonah on it, just going to be swallowed by the whale. Lawrence had written underneath: "Who is going to swallow whom?"

But I was still angry.

Finally Lawrence came from Capri, wanting to be back. The children tried like wise elders to talk me round. "Now Mrs. L." (so they called me) "be reasonable, you have married him, now you must stick to him."

So Lawrence came back. "Make yourself look nice to meet him," the children said. We met him at the station all dressed up. Then we all four had peace. He was charming with Else and Barby, trying to help them live their difficult young lives. "Else is not one of those to put the bed on fire, because there is a flea in it," Lawrence said of her.

But for his sister Ada he never felt the same again.

Villa Bernarda
Spotorno
Prov. di Genova
16 December 1925

My dear Mother-in-Law:

Soon Christmas comes again: here the children have written "natale" on every door. But it isn't a great fact in Italy. I was in Savona today: but you can't buy much there, not much of interest. I bought figs and dates and raisins, these are good. Tomorrow we will make a parcel for you of such things, I hope you get it in time for Christmas.

We are having lovely weather here again. Yesterday it wanted to snow, but this morning no such thing, only beautiful sunshine. My publisher Martin Secker is here, went to Savona with me. He is nice but not sparkling.

Now it is evening: we are sitting in the kitchen high under the roof. The evening star is white over the hill opposite, underneath the lights of the village lie like oranges and tangerines, little and shining. Frieda has devoured her whipped cream from Savona at one gulp, and now she moans that she hasn't kept any to eat with coffee and cake after supper. Now she sits by the stove and reads. The soup is boiling. In a moment we call down into the depth: "Vieni, Giovanni, é pronto il mangiare." Then the old man runs up the stairs like an unhappy frog, with his nose in the air, sniffing and smelling. It is nice for him to know that there is always something good for him to eat.

I am sending you a little money, you must always be the Duchess of the Stift. Be jolly.

D. H. L.

(Translated from the German)

VILLA BERNADA, SPOTORNO

VILLA BERNARDA
SPOTORNO
RIVIERA DI PONENTE
EASTER SUNDAY

My dear Mother-in-Law:

I am back. The three women were down at the station when I arrived yesterday, all dressed up festively, the women, not I. For the moment I am the Easter-lamb. When I went away, I was very cross, but one must be able to forget a lot and go on.

Frieda has a cold but Else and Barby have grown much stronger and Barby has painted one or two quite good pictures. I also feel much better, almost like in the past, only a little bronchitis. But they say, an Englishman at forty is almost always bronchial.

We don't know yet what we want to do. We leave this house on the twentieth and perhaps we'll go to Perugia between Florence and Rome, for six or eight weeks. I think I would like to write a book about Umbria and the Etruscans, half travel-book, also scientific. Perhaps I'll do this. Then we come to you in June when finally, in God's name, the weather is fine. Here it's always grey and close, sirocco. I think it is boiling, but slowly comes the spring.

D. H. L.

(Translated from the German)

VILLA BERNARDA
SPOTORNO
GENOA
7 MARCH 1926

Dear Else:

I got back here on Saturday, and found your letter. Frieda has a bad cold, but the two girls are very well. They are nice girls really, it is Frieda, who, in a sense, has made a bad use of them, as far as I am concerned.

Frieda thinks to bring them to Baden-Baden for a day or two, at the beginning of May. I shall stay in Florence presumably: and probably Frieda will come back there. I have an idea I might like to roam round in Umbria for a little while, and look at the Etruscan things, which interest me.

Thank you very much for offering us Irschenhausen. But I don't think now that I shall come to Germany till about July, so for heaven's sake, don't disappoint the young Ehepaar. I am leaving my plans quite indefinite. I sent you Knopf's Almanac, I thought it would amuse you. He was inspired to it by the Insel Verlag Almanac. . . . These copies must cost *him three dollars each—and he just presents one to each of his authors. I also ordered you* again "*The Plumed Serpent.*"

I am glad you had a good time with Nusch—she is really very nice with me always. I am sorry she couldn't come here.

Will you go to the south of France with Alfred? I was at Monte Carlo and at Nice, but I couldn't stand it. I didn't like it at all. But it isn't expensive—pension at the Beau Séjour at

Monaco was fifty francs. They say that Bormes, a little place off the railway, is very nice, with a very good hotel—not far from Toulon.

I shall be glad when this stupid and muddled winter is at last over. The weather is still very heavy and overcast, sirocco, not nice. It feels as if an earthquake were brewing somewhere.

We leave this house on the twentieth, presumably for Florence. I hope you'll have a good holiday. Remember me to Friedel, and Marianne. Brett is sailing for America, for the ranch, at the end of the month. Tante cose.

D. H. L.

Lawrence wanted to go further into the heart of Italy. The Etruscan tombs and remains interested him. But the ranch too called him.

However the idea of having to struggle with immigration officials, thinking of his tuberculosis, scared him. So he went to Florence, with Else and Barby. After a short time they went back to England.

Friends told us of a villa to let in the country about Florence. So we took a car and went out by the Porta Federicana through dreary suburban parts till we came to the end of the tramline.

It was April, the young beans were green and the wheat and the peas up, and we drove into the old Tuscan landscape, that perfect harmony of what nature did and man made. It is quite unspoiled there still. Beyond Scandicci we passed two cypresses and went to the left on a small, little used road. On the top of one of those Tuscan little hills stood a villa. My heart went out to it. I wanted that villa. It was rather large, but so perfectly placed, with a panorama of the Valdarno in front, Florence on the left, and the umbrella-pine woods behind.

"I do hope it is this one that's to let," I said to Lawrence, and my wish was fulfilled; we could have the villa, we could live in the Mirenda. We were thrilled by the peasants who belonged to the podere . . . the Orsini, Bandelli, and Pini. The Orsini had a wild feud with the Bandelli. The Bandelli fascinated me; a loosely built, untamed father and easy-going mother, and two beautiful wild girls, Tosca and Lila, and three beautiful boys. . . . My special favourite was Dino, who was so gently grey-eyed and angelic, but you knew perfectly well how he would laugh at you behind your back. So polite he was, carrying parcels for me, such exquisite manners at ten years old! Then I discovered that he looked very pale and ill at times and they told me that he had a rupture, and, with the brutality of boys, he told me the boys at school jeered at him for it. So I went with him to Doctor Giglioli in Florence and poor Dino was to have an operation. His sisters and I took him to the hospital, first decking him out with new shirts and vests. He was miserable, but chiefly miserable because they had put him among the women, him, a maschio. He was put to bed and, when we left him there, he crept under the sheets and shook with misery. Alas, next day, who appeared at home? Dino! He had crept about the place, seen a man under an anæsthetic, and fled. It was like putting a wild creature into a hospital. Then we persuaded him to go back, chiefly by telling him that, once operated, no one could laugh at him any more. So back he went, this time he had made up his mind. He was a plucky boy, and afterwards they told me at the hospital how they had never had a better, braver patient. It was a jolly hospital, this Florence one, so human and friendly, not at all prisonlike or too much white starch of nurses, white tiles, whitewash, white paint about, that one's very blood turns white. No, there your friends came to see you, everybody took a friendly interest in everybody else; well, such is life, here we are ever so ill, one day, then we get ever so well again, and then we die; "Ah, signora, cosí é la vita." And after the operation Dino was a prouder and more important person that he had ever been in his life, with his chicken-broth and good foods, and his new vests and shirts and socks, and two hankies, and actually some eau de Cologne. And proudly he told his sisters, in superior knowledge, when they asked for the W.C.: "There is a thing, and you pull, you must pull, see?" They not having seen such an arrangement before!

Then Dino came home and he brought me flowers and fruit and we were very fond of each other, although he never felt quite at ease with me.

Our servant was Giulia, from the Pini family. There was the Pini father, a zio, and a poor old zia, who had been buried in an earthquake and occasionally had fits, and Pietro who also helped Giulia about the house, arriving each morning to feed the chickens and goats, and Stellina, the horse. Giulia had to cut the grass every day with a sickle to feed all the animals. In the morning she was barefoot and shabby, but in the afternoon, when she heard a motorcar with visitors, she would appear at the Mirenda in high-heeled shoes and a huge bow in her hair. We loved Giulia . . . never was anything too much for her, gay and amusing and wise, she was.

For the first time, there near Florence, I got the Italian, especially the Tuscan, feel of things. In Florence, the ancient unbroken flower of a culture made its deep mark on me. The Misericordia, how deep it impressed me, the voluntary, immediate effort to help one's neighbour in distress. And when people pass it the youngest and the oldest take off their hats to it. . . . To me this seems real culture. . . . The Misericordia dates from the twelfth century and was founded by a facchino, an interesting story in itself.

Oh, the strange, almost ferocious intelligence of the Florentines!

What a pleasure it was to walk from the villa Mirenda, and take the tram in Scandicci to Florence! The handsome Tuscan girls with their glossy, neatly done hair in the tram . . . a chicken, sitting, tenderly held by its owner in a red hankie, its destiny either a sick friend or the mercato. Bottles of wine are hidden from the Dazio men, men friends embrace each other, somebody sees a relation and yells something about the "pasta" for midday, and so on, while we sail gaily on for Florence. There we would rush to Orioli's shop, hear his news and all the news of our friends. We would each dash out and do our exciting shopping. Shopping in Florence was still fun, not the dreary large-store drudgery. . . . There are the paper shops, leather shops, scent shops, stuffs; one glorious shop sells nothing but ribbons, velvet and silk, all colours and sizes, spotted and gold and silver. Another shop, all embroidery silks. Then to have your shoes made is so comfortable . . . the shoemaker feels your foot more important than the measuring. And then the "48" . . . what didn't we buy at the "48"!

Marionettes and pots and pans, china and glasses and hammers and paints. We would collect our things at Orioli's and drive home with Pietro and Giulia, furnishing the great kitchen at the Mirenda so conveniently with a few pounds, Lawrence designing a large kitchen table and brackets from which the pots hung. We painted the shutters of the Mirenda, and the chairs, green; we put "stuoie," thick pale grass matting, on the red-tiled floor in the big sitting-room. We had a few Vallombrosa chairs, a round table, a piano, hired, a couch and an old seat. The walls were syringed white with the syringe one uses to put verderane on the vines . . . that was done fast, and the sun poured into the big room so still and hot. The only noises came from the peasants, calling or singing at their work, or the water being drawn at the well. Or best, and almost too fierce, were the nightingales singing away from early dawn, almost the clock round . . . an hour or two's rest at midday in the heat. The spring that first year was a revelation in flowers, from the first violets in the woods . . . carpets of them we found, and as usual in our walks we took joyful possession of the unspoiled, almost medieval country around us. By the stream in the valley were tufts of enormous primroses, where the willow trees had been blood red through the winter. On the edge of the umbrella-pine woods, in the fields, were red and purple big anemones, strange, narrow-pointed, red and yellow wild tulips, bee orchids and purple orchids, tufts of tight-scented lavender . . . flowers thick like velvety carpets, like the ground in a Fra Angelico picture.

Our carriage and the Stellina were so small, I felt like sitting in a doll's perambulator. One day I went shopping with Pietro in Scandicci, when he had tooth-ache; he wore a red hankie round his poor swollen cheek, and on top on the hankie perched a hat, a bit sideways, with the Italian chic in it. He was very sorry for himself, and so was I, but none of the people we passed seemed to think us a funny sight, and we must have been, in that tiny barroccino, Pietro with his tooth-ache and his hankie by my side.

The Italians are so natural, one has tooth-ache and why hide it? Pietro would tell me: "Si, signora, questa sera vado a fare all'amore con la mia fidanzata." The fidanzata had only one eye, she was pretty, but in a self-conscious way she always kept the side *with* the eye toward one.

Christmas came and I wanted to make a Christmas tree for all the peasants. I told Pietro: "Buy me a tree in Florence, when you go to market."

"What," he said, "buy a tree, signora? Ah, no, one doesn't buy a tree, I'll get the signora one from the prete's wood."

On Christmas Day, or rather Christmas Eve, at four in the morning I heard a whisper: "Signora! Signora!" under my window. I looked out and there was Pietro with a large beautiful tree. He brought it in and how Lawrence and I and Giulia and Pietro enjoyed trimming that tree. There were pine-cones on it and we put gold and silver paper around these cones and Pietro would yell: "Guarda, guarda, signora, che bellezza!" while Lawrence and I went on trimming the tree with a lot of shiny things bought at the "48"; silver threads that we called "Christ Child hair" when I was small, and also lots and lots of candies. The Christmas tree looked so beautiful in that big white empty room, not a bit Christian, and how the peasant children loved their cheap wooden toys and how carefully they handled them, so precious were they. They had never had toys before. The grown-ups loved it too. We had difficulty in making them all go home again.

Such a sweetness and perfection of successive flowering Florence meant to us. We walked in the afternoons, almost awed through so much unknown, unobtrusive loveliness . . . the white oxen so carefully ploughing, between the cypresses, and flowers in the wheat, and beans and peas and clover! At twilight we would come home and light our stove in the big sitting-room, the stove that had been there for centuries, used as it had been to keep the silkworms warm in the winter . . . now it warmed us. We had no pictures on the walls, but Maria Huxley had left some canvases behind and I said: "Let's have some pictures."

Then, mixing his paints himself, boldly and joyfully, Lawrence began to paint. I watched him for hours, absorbed, especially when he began a new one, when he would mix his paints on a piece of glass, paint with a rag and his fingers, and

Sanity { instinct
intuition
spirit

the English have never painted from intuition or instinct

Man has two selves: one unknown, vital, living from roots: the other the known self, like a picture in a mirror or the objects on a tray. People live from this latter. And this latter can only feel known feelings: and its only experience of liberation or freedom is in the experience of novelty, which is the clash of sensation and a katabolic process.

Fac-simile:

Sanity { *Instinct*
Intuition
Spirit

The English have never painted from intuition or instinct.

Man has two selves: one unknown, vital, living from roots: the other the known self, like a picture in a mirror or the objects on a tray. People live from this latter. And this latter can only feel known *feelings: and its only experience of liberation or freedom is in the experience of novelty, which is the clash of sensation and a katabolic process.*

his palm and his brushes. "Try your toes next," I would say. Occasionally, when I was cooking pigeons that tasted of wine because they had fed on the dregs of grapes from the wine-press, or washing, he would call me, and I would have to hold out an arm or a leg for him to draw, or tell him what I thought of his painting.

He enjoyed his painting . . . with what intensity he went for it! Then he wrote "Lady Chatterley." After breakfast—we had it at seven or so—he would take his book and pen and a cushion, followed by John the dog, and go into the woods behind the Mirenda and come back to lunch with what he had written. I read it day by day and wondered how his chapters were built up and how it all came to him. I wondered at his courage and daring to face and write these hidden things that people dare not write or say.

For two years "Lady Chatterley" lay in an old chest that Lawrence had painted a greeny yellow with roses on it, and often when I passed that chest, I thought: "Will that book ever come out of there?"

Lawrence asked me: "Shall I publish it, or will it only bring me abuse and hatred again?" I said: "You have written it, you believe in it, all right, then publish it." So one day we talked it all over with Orioli; we went to a little old-fashioned printer, with a little old printing shop where they had only enough type to do half the book—and "Lady Chatterley" was printed. When it was done, stacks and stacks of "Lady C . . . ," or Our Lady, as we called it—were sitting on the floor of Orioli's shop. There seemed such a terrific lot of them that I said in terror: "We shall never sell all these." A great many were sold before there was a row; first some did not arrive at their destination in America, then there came abuse from England . . . but it was done . . . his last great effort.

He had done it . . . and future generations will benefit, his own race that he loved and his own class, that is less inhibited, for he spoke out of them and for them, there in Tuscany, where the different culture of another race gave the impetus to his work.

One winter we went to Diablerets and stayed in a little chalet. Aldous Huxley and Maria, Julian Huxley and Juliette, and their children shared a big villa nearby. Maria read "Lady C." there and Juliette was shocked at first. But then it was meant to be a shock. I can see Aldous and Lawrence talking together by the fire. I remember Aldous patiently trying to teach me to ski, but my legs tied themselves into knots with the skis and I seemed to be most of the time sitting in the snow collecting my legs.

We went for picnics in the snow, the Huxleys skiing, Lawrence and I in a sledge. I saw Diablerets again later on in the summer—I didn't recognize it, so completely different it looked in the snow.

I think the greatest pleasure and satisfaction for a woman is to live with a creative man, when he goes ahead and fights—I found it so. Always when he was in the middle of a novel or writing I felt happy as if something were happening, there was a new thing coming into the world. Often before he conceived a new idea he was irritable and disagreeable, but when it had come, the new vision, he could go ahead, and was eager and absorbed.

We had a very hot summer that year and we wanted to go to the mountains. One hot afternoon Lawrence had gathered peaches in the garden and came in with a basket full of wonderful fruit—he showed them to me—a very little while after

LAWRENCE AT VILLA BERNADA IN SPOTORNO

FRIEDA, LAWRENCE, AND HUXLEY AT THE MIRENDA

he called from his room in a strange, gurgling voice; I ran and found him lying on his bed; he looked at me with shocked eyes while a slow stream of blood came from his mouth. "Be quiet, be still," I said. I held his head, but slowly and terribly the blood flowed from his mouth. I could do nothing but hold him and try to make him still and calm and send for Doctor Giglioli. He came, and anxious days and nights followed. In this great heat of July nursing was difficult—Giulia, all the peasants—helped in every possible way. The signor was so ill—Giulia got down to Scandicci at four in the morning and brought ice in sawdust in a big handkerchief, and milk, but this, even boiled straightaway, would be sour by midday. The Huxleys came to see him, Maria with a great bunch of fantastically beautiful lotus, and Giglioli every day, and Orioli came and helped. But I nursed him alone night and day for six weeks, till he was strong enough to take the night train to the Tyrol.

This was another inroad his illness made. We both fought hard and won.

People came to see us at the Mirenda. Capitano Ravagli had to come to Florence for a military case—he came to see us and showed Lawrence his military travel-pass. When Lawrence saw on it: *Capitano Ravagli* deve *partire* (must *leave*) *at such and such a time* . . . he shook his head and said resentfully: "Why must? why must? there shouldn't be any *must*. . . ."

One Sunday afternoon Osbert and Edith Sitwell came. They moved us strangely. They seemed so oversensitive, as if something had hurt them too much, as if they had to keep up a brave front to the world, to pretend they didn't care and yet they only cared much too much. When they left, we went for a long walk, disturbed by them. But how afterwards they could think that "Lady Chatterley" had anything to do with them, is beyond me. "Lady Chatterley" was written and finished before Lawrence ever set eyes on any Sitwell.

That autumn we gave up the Mirenda. Lawrence had been so ill there and wanted the sea. I went to pack up at the Mirenda, it was a grief to me. I had been so very happy there except for Lawrence's illness. How great the strain was at times, always the strain of his health. The last ounce of my strength seemed to be drained at times but I had my reward. He got better and I always knew however tired I might be he felt worse than ever I could. Making another effort my own strength grew. I never had time to think of my own health, so it looked after itself and it never let me down. The peasants at the Mirenda, the very place itself, the woods with their umbrella-pines, the group of buildings, seemed sad at being left.

The peasants took all the belongings we had collected and carried them away on their backs, like gnomes they crept under their loads down the path. When I gave a last look from the two cypress trees along the road there stood the Mirenda upon its hill in the evening sun, with its shutters closed, old and solid, it seemed as if its eyes had closed for sleep, to dream of the life that had been and gone.

Lawrence had gone to Port Cros with Richard Aldington, Brigit Patmore, and Dorothy Yorke—Arabella we called her.

I joined them there. Port Cros seemed an island of mushrooms—I had never seen so many as there on the moist warm ground of the undergrowth. We had a donkey and a man who worked for us and brought up the food from the little harbour below. Lawrence was not well and I remember how we all did our best on the top of that island to help him in every way.

We drank coffee in the inner space of the small fortress we lived in. The donkey looked on and Richard jumped up to play the brave toreador, waving his blue scarf at the donkey. Jasper was its name. Jasper fled into the bushes but its long ears stuck out and he had to peep at Richard—he hadn't got the bullfight idea, but was intrigued.

Richard was an education in itself to me: he knew so much about Napoleon, for instance, and made me see Napoleon from a different angle, the emotional power he had over his men. Richard told me of his war experiences, death experience and beyond death: it seemed to melt one's brain away; Richard began writing his "Death of a Hero" there in Port Cros. One day we went bathing in the bluest little bay, when an octopus persecuted Brigit and Richard had to beat it away.

We wanted to go to the mainland, not to be so far away with Lawrence so frail. So we left for Toulon, gay Toulon with its ships and sailors and shops, real sailors' shops, with boxes adorned with shells, ships made of shells, long knives from Corsica, on which was written: "Che la mia ferita sia mortale."

Near Toulon, at Bandol, in the hotel Beau Rivage we stayed all winter. A sunny hotel by the sea, friendly and easy as only Provence can be. We seemed to live completely the life of a "petit rentier," as Rousseau le Douanier has painted it. Lawrence wrote "Pansies" in his room in the morning, then we went to have our apéritif before lunch in a café on the sea-front. There was a small war memorial, a gay young damsel that would please any poilu. We knew all the dogs of the small place, we saw the boats come in, their silvery loads of sardines glittering on the sand of the shores. Lawrence was better that winter in health. He watched the men playing "boccia" on the shore, after lunch. We seemed to share the life of the little town, running along so easily. We went with the bus to Toulon. We saw the coloured soldiers. We went to a beautiful circus. Yes, easy and sunny was this winter in Bandol.

The Huxleys came and later on they found a house across the bay at Sanary. I see us sitting in the sunny dining-room of the Beau Rivage, and Lawrence saying to Maria: "No, Maria, you would not be a bit nice if you were really very rich."

In the spring we went to Spain from Marseilles—to Barcelona, from there to Mallorca. Mallorca still has a depth to it, a slight flavour of Africa, a distance in its horizon over the sea.

Our hotel was by a small bay. Deliciously hot, the days went by. We went all over the island, always wary not to tire Lawrence. I bathed in the heat of midday and climbed the rocks with the little bay entirely to myself. But one day I looked around and saw a Spanish officer on a splendid horse, looking out towards the sea; I was disturbed in my loneliness and wanted to dash to my bathing cloak and go away. I sprang on to a heap of seaweeds that had a hole underneath it and rocks. Like a gunshot my ankle snapped, I collapsed sick with pain. The officer rode up and offered me his horse that danced about. I thought: what a waste of a romantic situation; the ankle hurts so much, I can't get on to a prancing horse—if I could only be alone with this pain.

Lawrence appeared, got two young men to take me to the hotel in their car. The ankle did not hurt any more, but it was broken.

Lawrence wanted me to go to London to be there for the

exhibition of his paintings. A gay flag with his name was flying outside the Warren Gallery when I went there. His pictures looked a little wild and overwhelming in the elegant, delicate rooms of the galleries. But never could I have dreamed that a few pictures could raise such a storm. I had not realized their potency in the big, bare rooms of the Mirenda, where they had been born so naturally, as if Tuscany had given its life to them. I was astonished. Then the Police came and put them in the cellar of Marlborough Police station to be destroyed. I was worried lest the cellar be damp and so destroy them that way. But no, they were saved; it was a fight, though.

Meanwhile Lawrence was ill in Florence. What with the abuse of "Lady Chatterley" and the disapproval of the pictures, he had become ill. Orioli telegraphed in distress. So off I set on my journey to Florence, my ankle still wabbly and aching and with constant worry in my mind of how I would find Lawrence. Orioli told me that after receiving my telegram saying I was coming, he had said: "What will Frieda say when she arrives?" And Lawrence had answered: "Do you see those peaches in the bowl? She will say, 'What lovely peaches,' and she will devour them." So it was. After my first look at Lawrence, when his eyes had signalled to me their relief, "She is here with me," I felt my thirst from the long journey and ate the peaches.

He always got better when I was there. But Orioli told me how scared he had been when he had seen Lawrence, his head and arms hanging over the side of the bed, like one dead.

We left the heat of Florence for the Tegernsee to be near Max Mohr. We had a rough peasant house, it was autumn. Lawrence rested a great deal. My sister Else came to see him, and Alfred Weber. When he was alone with Alfred Weber, he said to him: "Do you see those leaves falling from the apple tree? When the leaves want to fall you must let them fall." Max Mohr had brought some doctors from Munich, but medicine did not help Lawrence. His organism was too frail and sensitive. I remember some autumn nights when the end seemed to have come. I listened for his breath through the open door, all night long, an owl hooting ominously from the walnut tree outside. In the dim dawn an enormous bunch of gentians I had put on the floor by his bed seemed the only living thing in the room. But he recovered and slowly Max Mohr and I travelled with him south again to Bandol.

After the Mirenda we seemed to live chiefly for his health. Switzerland and the sea one after the other seemed to do him most good. He did not want any doctors or cures. "I know so much better about myself than any doctor," he would say. His life became a struggle for health. And yet he would rise above it so amazingly and his spirit brought forth immortal flowers right up to the very end. One of his desires was to write a novel about each continent. Africa and Asia still he wanted to do. It was not given to him to do so. As one of my Indian friends here said: "Why didn't Mr. Lawrence write about the whole world? He knew all about it." When he had read "The Lost Girl" he said: "What happened to those people afterwards? I want to know their story till they die."

Here these Indians seem to understand him so immediately —better, I believe, than his white fellowmen.

The Nightingale

by D. H. Lawrence

Tuscany is full of nightingales, and in spring and summer they sing all the time, save in the middle of the night and the middle of the day. In the little leafy woods that hang on the steep of the hill toward the streamlet, as maidenhair hangs on a rock, you hear them piping up in the wanness of dawn, about four o'clock in the morning: Hello! Hello! Hello! It is the brightest sound, perhaps, of all sounds in the world: a nightingale piping up. Every time you hear it, you feel a wonder and, it must be confessed, a thrill, because the sound is so bright, so glittering, and it has such power behind it.

"There goes the nightingale!" you say to yourself: and it is as if the stars were darting up from the little thicket and leaping away into the vast vagueness of the sky, to be hidden and gone. And every single time you hear the nightingale afresh, your second thought is: "Now *why* do they say he is a sad bird?"

He is the noisiest, most inconsiderate, most obstreperous and jaunty bird in the whole kingdom of birds. How John Keats managed to begin his "Ode to a Nightingale" with "My heart aches, and a drowsy numbness pains my senses . . ."—well, I for one don't know. You can hear the nightingale silverily shouting: "What? What? What, John? Heart aches and a drowsy numbness pains?—tra-la-la!-tri-li-lily-lilyly!"

And why the Greeks said he—or she—was sobbing in a bush for a lost lover, again I don't know. Jug-jug-jug! say the medieval writers, to represent the rolling of the little balls of lightning in the nightingale's throat. A wild rich sound, richer than the eyes in a peacock's tail.

"And the bright brown nightingale, amorous,
Is half assuaged for Itylus—"

They say, with that jug! jug! jug! that she is sobbing. It really is mysterious, what people hear. You'd think they had their ears on upside down. Anyone who ever heard the nightingale "sobbing" must have quite a different hearing-faculty from the one I've got.

Anyhow, it's a male sound, a most intensely and undilutedly male sound. And pure assertion. There is not a hint nor shadow of echo and hollow recall. Nothing at all like a hollow low bell. Nothing in the world so unforlorn.

Perhaps that is what made Keats straightway feel forlorn.

Forlorn! the very word is like a bell
To toll me back from thee to my sole self!

Perhaps that is the reason of it: why they all hear sobs in the bush, where any really normal listening mortal hears the silver ringing shouts of cherubim. Perhaps because of the discrepancy.

Because, as a matter of fact, the nightingale sings with a ringing, punching vividness and a pristine assertiveness that makes a mere man sit down and consider. It is the kind of brilliant calling and interweaving of glittering exclamation which must have been heard on the first day of creation, when the angels suddenly found themselves created in brightness, and found themselves able to shout aloud. Then there must have been a nightingaleish to-do! Hello! Hello! Behold!

Behold! Behold! It is I! It is I! What a mar-mar-marvellous occurrence! What?

For the pure splendid splendidness of vocal assertion: *Lo! It is I!* you have to listen to the nightingale. Perhaps for the visual perfection of the same assertion, you have to look at a peacock shaking all his eyes. Among all creatures created in positive splendour, these two are perhaps the most perfect: the one in invisible, triumphing sound, the other in voiceless visibility. The nightingale is a quite undistinguished grey-brown bird, if you do see him: although he's got that tender, hopping mystery about him, of a thing that is rich alive inside. Just as the peacock, when he does make himself heard, is awful, but still impressive: such a fearful shout from out of the menacing jungle. You can actually see him, in Ceylon, yell from a high bough, then stream away past the monkeys, into the impenetrable jungle that seethes and is dark.

And, perhaps, for this reason—the reason, that is, of pure angel-keen self-assertion—the nightingale makes a man feel sad, and the peacock so often makes him feel angry. Because they are so triumphantly positive in their created selves, eternally new from the hand of the rich bright God, and perfect. The nightingale simply ripples with his own perfection. And the peacock arches all his bronze and purple eyes with assuredness.

This, this rippling assertion of perfection, this emerald shimmer of a perfect self, makes men angry or melancholy, according as it assails the eye or the ear. The ear is much less cunning than the eye. You can say to somebody: I like you awfully: you look so beautiful this morning! and they'll believe it utterly, though your voice may really be vibrating with mortal hatred. The ear is so stupid, it will accept any amount of false money in words. But let one tiny gleam of the mortal hatred come into your eye, or across your face, and it will be detected instantly. The eye is so shrewd and rapid.

For this reason, we see the peacock at once, in his showy male self-assertion: and we say, rather sneeringly: Fine feathers make fine birds! But when we hear the nightingale, we don't know what we hear, we only know we feel sad: forlorn! And so we say it is the nightingale that is sad.

The nightingale, let us repeat, is the most unsad thing in the world: even more unsad than the peacock full of gleam. The nightingale has nothing to be sad about. He feels perfect with life. It isn't conceit. He just feels life perfect, and he trills it out, shouts, jugs, gurgles, calls, declares, asserts, and triumphs, but never reflects. It is pure music, in so far as you could never put words to it. But there are words for the feelings aroused in us by the song. No! even that is not true. There are no words to tell what one really feels, hearing the nightingale. It is something so much more pure than words. But it is some sort of feeling of triumph in one's own life perfection. Keats feels this all, through his ode.

'Tis not through envy of thy happy lot,
But being too happy in thy happiness,—
That thou, light-wingèd Dryad of the trees,
In some melodious plot
Of beechen green, and shadows numberless,
Singest of summer in full-throated ease . . .

It is beautiful poetry, of a truthful poet. And Keats keeps it up, in the next stanza, wanting to drink the blushful Hippocrene and fade away with the nightingale into the forest dim.

Fade far away, dissolve, and quite forget
What thou among the leaves hast never known,
The weariness, the fever, and the fret . . .

It is such lovely poetry! But the next line is a bit ridiculous, so I won't quote it. Yes, I will:

Here, where men sit and hear each other groan;
Where palsy shakes a few, sad, last grey hairs . . . etc.

This is Keats, not the nightingale.—But Keats still tries to break away, and get over into the nightingale world.

Away! away! for I will fly to thee,
Not charioted by Bacchus and his pards,
But on the viewless wings of Poesy . . .

He doesn't succeed, however. The viewless wings of Poesy carry him only into the bushes, not into the nightingale world. He is still outside.

Darkling I listen; and for many a time
I have been half in love with easeful Death . . .

I am sure the sound of the nightingale never made any man in love with easeful death—except by contrast. The contrast between the bright flame of positive pure self-perfection, in the bird, and the uneasy flame of waning selflessness, for ever reaching out to be something not himself, in the poet!

To cease upon the midnight with no pain,
While thou art pouring forth thy soul abroad
In such an ecstasy!
Still wouldst thou sing, and I have ears in vain—
To thy high requiem become a sod.

How astonished the nightingale would be if he could be made to realize what sort of answer the poet was answering to his song! He would fall off the bough with amazement.

Because a nightingale, when you answer him back, only

shouts and sings louder. Suppose a few other nightingales pipe up in the neighbouring bushes—as they always do—then the blue-white sparks of sound go dazzling up to heaven. And suppose you, mere mortal, happen to be sitting on the shady bank having an altercation with the mistress of your heart, hammer and tongs, then the chief nightingale swells and goes it like Caruso in the third act, simply a brilliant, bursting frenzy of music, singing you down: till you simply can't hear yourself speak to quarrel, and you have to laugh.

There was, in fact, something very like a nightingale in Caruso, that bird-like bursting miraculous energy of song and self-utterance, and self-luxuriance.

Thou wast not born for death, immortal Bird!
No hungry generations tread thee down . . .

Not yet in Tuscany, anyhow. They are twenty to the dozen. And the cuckoo seems remote and low-voiced, calling low, half-secretive, even as he flies past.—Perhaps really it is different in England.

The voice I heard this passing night was heard
In ancient days by emperor and clown:
Perhaps the self-same song that found a path
Through the sad heart of Ruth, when, sick for home,
She stood in tears amid the alien corn.

I wonder what sort of answer they all made! Diocletian, for instance! And Æsop! And Mademoiselle Ruth! I strongly suspect the last young lady of giving the nightingale occasion to sing, like the nice damsel in the Boccaccio story, who went to sleep with the nightingale in her hand: "tua figliuola é stata si vaga dell'usignuolo, che ella l'ha preso e tienlosi in mano."

And I wonder what the hen nightingale thinks of it all, as she mildly sits upon the eggs and hears milord giving himself forth? Probably she likes it, for she goes on breeding him true to type. Probably she likes it better than if, like the poet, he humbly warbled:

Now more than ever seems it rich to die,
To cease upon the midnight with no pain . . .

One sympathizes with Keats's Fanny, and understands why she wasn't having any. Much *she'd* have got out of such a midnight! Perhaps, when all's said and done, the female of the species prefers it when the male of the species is full of his own bright life, and warbles her into the spell of himself. In the end, she gets more out of it that way.

Because, of course, though the nightingale is utterly unconscious of the little dim hen while he sings, *she* knows well enough that the song is half her; just as the eggs are half his. And just as she doesn't want him coming and putting a heavy foot down on her little bunch of eggs, he doesn't want her to go nestling down on his song and smothering it, or muffling it. Every man to his trade, and every woman to hers.

Adieu! adieu! thy plaintive anthem fades . . .

It never was a plaintive anthem, it was Caruso at his best. But don't argue with a poet.

VILLA MIRENDA
SCANDICCI
FIRENZE
26 MARCH 1926

My dear Else:

The Schwiegermutter wrote from Baden that you aren't well, and had a little operation. That's bad luck! I do hope you're better.

It isn't a good year, anyhow. Here it has rained and rained, till the country is turning yellow with wetness. But these last two days are sunny and warm: but not hot, as it should be.

We took the top half of this old villa, out on one of the little hills of Tuscany, about seven miles from Florence. We are two kilometres from the tram, which takes us in to the Duomo in half an hour. The country around is pretty—all poderi and pinewoods, and no walls *at all. I hope in the autumn, really, you'll come and stay a while: unless everything goes muddled again. For myself, I struggle to get back into a good humour, but don't succeed very well.—We've got the villa for a year, anyhow, so there should be time.*

Myself, I am labouring at the moment to type Frieda's MS. of the play "David." It's a slow business, I'm no typist. But it is just as well for me to go through the MS. myself and it is good for me to learn some German, I suppose.

Frieda's daughter Else typed the first twenty-six pages and there are a fair number of alterations. But I shall send you the typescript as soon as it is finished: within a month, pray God!—

I am interested, really, to see the play go into German, so much simpler and more direct than in English. English is really very complicated in its meanings. *Perhaps the simpler a language becomes in its grammar and syntax, the more subtle and complex it becomes in its suggestions. Anyhow, this play seems to me much more direct and dramatic in German, much less poetic and suggestive than in English. I shall be interested to know what you think of it.*

I said to myself I would write perhaps a book about the Etruscans: nothing pretentious, but a sort of book for people who will actually be going to Florence and Cortona and Perugia and Volterra and those places, to look at the Etruscan things. They have a great attraction for me: there are lovely things in the Etruscan Museum here, which no doubt you've seen. But I hope you'll come in the autumn and look at them again with me. Mommsen hated everything Etruscan, said the germ of all degeneracy was in the race. But the bronzes and terracottas are fascinating, so alive with physical life, with a powerful physicality which surely is as great, or sacred, ultimately, as the ideal *of the Greeks and Germans. Anyhow, the real strength of Italy seems to me in this physicality, which is not at all Roman. —I haven't yet seen any of the painted tombs at . . . !*

GRAND HOTEL
CHEXBRES-SUR-VEVEY
SUNDAY MORNING

Had your p.c. this morning—glad you found Nusch there. I guess you'll schwätzen schwätzen all the day. Today is better here—am sitting on my little balcony to write this—Achsah has already sent Earl down with a cup of Ovaltine—and it is sunny in snatches. I worked over my Isis story a bit—am going to try it on Earl. Last night we sang songs, Twankydillo, etc., up in Achsah's attic. Everything very quiet and domestic.

Had a few letters forwarded from Florence this morning: enclose the Curtis Brown. Ask Else what she thinks about a complete break in November with Insel Verlag. Of course it is insolence on their part that they won't tell my agents what they are doing with my books. They should of course write Miss Watson about the proposed book of short stories. Ask Else about it—what they are really doing. And ask her if she kept that short biography of me which she did for the "Frankfurter Zeitung" man. If she did, you might look it over and send it to Miss Watson, in English, *for this Kra man. I simply can't write biographies about myself. Damn them all.*

A sort of lamentable letter from Cath Carswell—no money, etc.—and still fussing about what Yvonne Franchetti said about that typing. Then a letter from the irrepressible Durham miner man—wanting "Lady C." very much—nothing else—no word from Orioli though it's his handwriting on the envelopes. Nothing from Huxleys either, save their telegram. Madame will have a double room for them. Wish they'd bring their car, we could look at places a bit higher. I told you they arrive next Tuesday or Wednesday. There is nothing forwarded from that St.-Nizier place.

I think of you in the Schwiegermutter's room, with Nusch there. Has die Anna got any flowers? Buy her a nice pot from me. And buy something for Nusch for twenty marks. I want her to have something for a quid. Only not Schnecken or foie gras. I now smell Braten of some sort. Perhaps we shall go to Vevey this afternoon. We want to go to Gruyère when you come back—also to Le Pont, which is M. Stucke's other hotel about three thousand feet up, with three little lakes. Might go there. But he leases it in summer to another hotelier. What are Nusch's plans? Love to you all—the goddesses three.

D. H. L.

AT BAILATHADAN
NEWTONMORE
INVERNESS
20 AUGUST 1926

Dear Else:

Frieda sent me on your letter from Irschenhausen. I am glad you like being there, but am surprised it is so cold. Here the weather is mild, mixed rainy and sunny. The heather is out on the moors: the day lasts till nine o'clock: yet there is that dim, twilight feeling of the North. We made an excursion to the west, to Fort William and Mallaig, and sailed up from Mallaig to the Isle of Skye. I liked it very much. It rains and rains, and the white wet clouds blot over the mountains. But we had one perfect day, blue and iridescent, with the bare northern hills sloping green and sad and velvety to the silky blue sea. There is still something of an Odyssey up there, in among the islands and the silent lochs: like the twilight morning of the world, the herons fishing undisturbed by the water, and the sea running far in, for miles, between the wet, trickling hills, where the cottages are low and almost invisible, built into the earth. It is still out of the world, and like the very beginning of Europe: though, of course, in August there are many tourists and motorcars. But the country is almost uninhabited.

I am going south, tomorrow, to stay with my sisters in Lincolnshire for a little while, by the sea. Then really I should like to come to Bavaria, if only for a fortnight. I have a feeling that I want to come again to Bavaria. I hope I shan't have to stay in

England for that play. I would much rather come to Germany at the end of August. And Frieda, I know, has had enough, more than enough, of London. Perhaps after all we can come to Irschenhausen for the first part of September, and let that inhalation wait a while.—I am much better since I am here in Scotland: it suits me here: and probably the altitude of Irschenhausen would suit me too. Anyhow we could go back to Baden to do a bit of inhaling. There is no hurry to get to Italy.—If only I need not stay in London for that play.

I find it most refreshing to get outside the made world, if only for a day—like to Skye. It restores the old Adam in one. The made world is too deadening—and too dead.

So I am still hoping to see you all—Friedel will be there?—in Bayern, quite soon. Why should one be put off, from what one wants to do.

Auf Wiedersehen.

D. H. L.

DUNEVILLE
TRUSTHORPE RD.
SUTTON-ON-SEA, LINCS.
7 SEPTEMBER 1926

My dear Else:

I had your letter today. I'm very disappointed not to be able to come to Irschenhausen. Those fools are still delaying beginning the play. We go to London on Saturday—I'm not sure of the address—and I shall see what I can do. But I am annoyed and bored beforehand.

But I doubt if we could get to Bavaria before the end of the month. Too late! I shall have to wait till spring, and go straight to Irschenhausen from Italy, if I may.

I expect we shall be in Baden, at least a day or two—travel over Paris. So we shall see you. I do hope you are feeling better. What makes you so knocked up?

It's dull weather here—a grey sky, a grey sea. My thoughts are turning south. The swifts are already going, and the swallows are gathering to go. Nothing to stay for.

Auf Wiedersehen.

D. H. L.

Villa Mirenda
Scandicci
Florence
12 October 1926

Dear Else:

I have just had the enclosed letter from my agent. My agreement with him is such, that the contracts for all the things I publish must be made through him, and all payments must be made to him. He deducts ten per cent for himself, and deposits the rest to my account.

Will you please tell me what contract you made with the Insel Verlag for "Der Fuchs": and what were the payments, apart from the translator's fee? I know it was not much. But of course I owe Curtis Brown ten per cent on it.

And in future will you see that everything goes through the agent's hands, or I shall be in trouble, as I am legally bound to him: he is quite good to me. It's my fault, I know, for not remembering sooner.

We have been back here just a week, and I am very glad to sit still in the peace of these quiet rooms. I am getting really tired of moving about, and cast round in my mind for a place which I shall keep as a permanency. Perhaps it will be in England.

It is warm here, almost hot still. The vendemmia finished last week, and we are all festooned with grapes. But the Schwiegermutter says that you too were in Venice. Venice is lovely in autumn, if it's not too crowded. Do you feel content now, for the winter?

They are producing the "David" play in December. I saw the producer and the people concerned, and I promised to go to England to help them at the end of November. I am not very *sure if I shall do so, though. But if we do, we must come through Baden. I daren't say anything, because I know the Schwiegermutter was cross with us for putting off again this time. But we had moved so much, we were both feeling stupefied.*

I wonder how the translation of the "Serpent" is going. You will find it a long job: I hope not too tedious. Myself, I am not working at anything particular: don't feel inclined.

I hope you are feeling well. Are the children all busy again, Friedel in Berlin? Here it seems so sleepy—the world is all vague.

Love,

D. H. L.

VILLA MIRENDA
SCANDICCI
FIRENZE
18 OCTOBER 1926

Dear Else:

Kippenberg behaves as if he were the great Chan of Tartary: whereas he's only a tiresome old buffer. I have told him that once personally, I don't care for Franzius's pompous and heavy translation: I'll tell him again, and to hell with him. Pity we can't change over to the people who did "Jack in Bushland." They are more up to date and go-ahead.

But anyhow Kip has no right over magazine productions: so if you could get "The Woman Who Rode Away" into a Monatsheft, you couldn't be interfered with, by him at least. I get awfully bored, between publishers and agents, and one state and another.

So now you'll be off to Vienna! Everybody seems to have been to Vienna, or to be going. Glad I needn't go, anyhow just now.

I'll tell Curtis Brown what you say about "Fox."

Sunny autumn here, still and nice: but an epidemic of typhoid in the neighbourhood: must look out.

I feel I'll never write another novel: that damned old Franzius turning "The Plumed Serpent" into a ponderous boa constrictor! O Germania! It really is time you bobbed your philosophic hair!

Wiedersehen,

D. H. L.

IRSCHENHAUSEN
SUNDAY

My dear Else:

Many thanks for the pen, which I am so glad to have in my fingers again—it's an old friend: it wrote "Boy in the Bush" and "St. Mawr" and "Princess" and "Woman Who Rode Away" and "Plumed Serpent" and all the stories in between: not bad, even if it is a nasty orangy brown colour. But I've got even to like this colour. They seem to have mended it all right, it goes well.

This is the horridest day of all, after tea and still pouring with rain: and I would like to go out! If only I had strong boots and a rain-proof. I would of course if we were staying. —Yesterday was lovely and sunny till teatime.

This weekend we are alone—Anna is coming tomorrow. Then I suppose the Meyers will come and the Kahlers—and I've promised to go to Schoenberner's, and to meet Hans Carossa there. I heard from England that a man who writes plays and thinks I am the greatest living novelist (quote) and who lives in Tegernsee, may come and see me: Max Mohr: do you know anything about him? I don't.

I began the little bag—with green grass waves and dandelion seed-stones—you know, the fluffy balls—and it's going to have bees. But today is so dark and the stuff is so black! But it will be rather a small bag.

I suppose we shall stay here till Monday week—is that December 2nd? I don't feel a bit anxious to return to Italy—but

I think Frieda does. I don't mind, for the time being, if it rains and is dark.—By the way, you should see how pretty your garden looks, with the gold, and the mauve of the Michaelmas daisies, and the big autumn daisy, and the pink phlox: it looks really gay, on a sunny day.—We have gathered the apples—so bright and red—and the last two hazel-nuts, I'm afraid either squirrels or children had fetched the others. The woods are simply populated with mushrooms, all sorts, in weird camps everywhere—really like strange inhabitants come in. We eat the little yellow ones, and keep picking Steinpilze and throwing them away again. The cows come every afternoon on to our grass, with a terrific tintinnabulation, like a host of tinkling Sundays. There is a Jersey who is pining to come to tea in the porch—and a white calf that suddenly goes round the moon. Frieda reads Goethe, and I play patience—today I have finished my "Cavalleria Rusticana" translation: now I've only to do the introduction: if that fool of a young postman hasn't lost my bookful of MS. that I sent to England. Frieda told him loudly registered; *he says he sent it unregistered—and Drucksache. I shall curse him if I have to do it all over again.*

It's nightfall—I think I shall go out, spite of rain, for a few minutes.

Wiedersehen!

D. H. L.

VILLA MIRENDA
SCANDICCI
FLORENCE
10 JANUARY 1927

Dear Else:

That was a nice letter you wrote—and a very nice little purse you sent me for Christmas. I ought to have thanked you before—but something has happened to me about letters—in fact all writing. I seem to be losing my will-to-write altogether: in spite of the fact that I am working at an English novel—but so differently from the way I have written before!

I spend much more time painting—have already done three, nearly four, fairly large pictures. I wonder what you'll say to them when you'll see them. Painting is more fun than writing, much more of a game, and costs the soul far, far less.

I enclose a cross letter from Curtis Brown's foreign clerk. I have answered that I don't believe you have made any legal agreement whatsoever with Insel Verlag. Have you? Do let me know. It is rather a bore, the high-handed way old Kippenberg behaves, as if he were the great Chan of publishers. I should like to get a bit of a slap at him.

It's very nice that Alfred is being feasted and rejoiced over. Congratulate him for me. It is *nice to have a bit of grateful recognition, whatever one may say.*

I am going to make another effort to get the two downstairs rooms with the big terrace, so you could have them as a little apartment when you come. They would be so nice.

They keep deferring the production of "David"—no doubt they are frightened of it. I believe they hated "The Widowing of Mrs. Holroyd." Now they say "David" will probably be April, but I don't mind, because I'd much rather stay here till the sun warms up a bit in the north. . . . One gets sick of winter . . . though it is a lovely day today.

Auf Wiedersehen then,

D. H. L.

Villa Mirenda
Florence
Wednesday evening

Dear Mother-in-Law:

Frieda and I arrived at the same moment at the station in Milan, the two trains at the same time, and the two porters brought us together in two minutes. Wasn't that clever?

We have just entered the Villa Mirenda, all good and lovely here! friends with flowers, and the peasants all there to welcome us, very nice and friendly. Now we have eaten and sit by the fire for an hour, then to bed.

Frieda is happy to be back, goes about and looks at everything. Nice is the tie. I must look at the colour in the daytime. I'm so glad you're well. I'm coming in the spring and we'll eat strawberries and cream, shan't we?

Such lovely primulas and violets on the table under the lamp. Good night then.

D. H. L.

Friends are going to Florence tomorrow and will put this letter in the post. I want you to know that we arrived safely.

(Translated from the German)

VILLA MIRENDA
SCANDICCI
FLORENCE
14 APRIL 1927

My dear Mother-in-Law:

I am home again—I returned Monday evening from Volterra. I had a very beautiful week with Brewster. We went to Cerveteri, Tarquinia, and Vulci, Grosseto and Volterra, not far from the sea, north of Rome. The Etruscan tombs are very interesting and so nice and lovable. They were a living, fresh, jolly people, lived their own lives without wanting to dominate the lives of others. I am fond of my Etruscans—they had life in themselves, so they had no need to govern others. I want to write some sketches of these Etruscan places, not scientifically, but only as they are now and the impression they make.

I found Frieda with a cold and a little depressed, but she is well again and herself once more. Barby came Tuesday with Mrs. Seaman—she is nice, older than last year, not so beautiful, tall as a telegraph pole, quieter, not much life in her. That is London over one. She will stay here three weeks. She works well in her school and really wants to be free, but it will take another year and a half at least. But it is better that she works. If she had much money and were quite free, it would be worse. Oh, liberty, liberty, what have you done for poor woman! But they must go on to spread their bread of life with that poison, poison of liberty.

The weather, thank God, is always lovely. There are still

tulips in the corn and apple and peach blossoms. The peasants are faithful and nice. The house is still. It is good to be here. Frieda has gone to Scandicci—Barby and Mrs. Seaman to Florence—so I am alone.

I am wearing the socks you knitted me, they are beautiful and exactly the colour of my trousers, very elegant. And the ties are beautiful—I tried the speckled one at once. I am glad you are so well and your Stift is always made more beautiful. The world goes forward, surely.

Later on, we will make plans for the summer, when and how to come. I don't want to think of travel, it is enough. Greet Else when you see her. Frieda has come home from Alassio with the love for her sister all new and shiny again. Good! Greet the ladies, my friends. When I come, we will eat Blaufelchen. There is no fish as good in Italy.

Then farewell,

D. H. L.

(Translated from the German)

VILLA MIRENDA
SCANDICCI
FLORENCE
1 JUNE 1927

My dear Else:

Could you get me a copy of F. Weege's "Etruskische Malerei"—costs about twenty marks—at least, in England twenty. If the bookseller can get me a copy, and send it me here by registered post—else they'll steal it—Drucksache, I shall be very glad, and will send you the money at once, when you let me know how much it was. It is a nice book—very—I saw it at a friend's house—and should like to have it. I heard when I was in Tarquinia that Weege was in Florence—but not doing any more Etruscan books.

It is very hot here, too hot—to sit in the sun for breakfast, even before seven in the morning. One gets up early, then has a siesta in the afternoon. Frieda is still peacefully slumbering—I have wakened up early from mine—and not a soul is alive on all the poderi—peasants sleeping too. The Arno valley lies hot and still, in the sun, but there is a little breeze, so I shall go down and sit on the grass in a deck chair under the nespole tree. The nespole are just ripe—I shall climb up and get the first today—warm—they are good like that. The big cherries also are ripe—Giulia brings them in—very good. It seems to me always very pleasant when it is full summer and one ceases to bother about anything, goes drowsy, like an insect.

We heard from friends that the performance of "David"

went off very well, and the play was well received. But the notices in the newspapers are very contrary. They say the play was very dull, that it was like a cinema with too much talking, that it was boring and no drama in it, and that it was a very great mistake for a clever man like me to offer such a thing for the actual stage. A clever man like me doesn't fret over what they say. If the producers made a bad film of it, that's the producers' fault. And if the dramatic critics can only listen to snappy talk about divorces and money, that's their fault too. They should pray to the Lord—"Lend thou the listening ear" and not blame me. Anyhow, io ne mi frego! Frieda, however, was very disappointed and downcast about it and almost refused to be comforted. We shall hear more later.

Unless it gets sizzling hot, I suppose we shall stay here till towards the end of July. We may do a little giro to Cortona and Arezzo and Chiusi and Orvieto, coming back by Assisi and Perugia: if it's not too hot. Then for August we can go to Baden to the Schwiegermutter—that hot and tiresome month, when everybody in the whole world is somewhere where they shouldn't be. Did you say you were going to the Haute Savoie? That'll be very nice—I have got some friends gone there just now. If it weren't the wrong time of year, a bit too warm for you—I should suggest you bring the children here and make use of this flat while we are away, and the young ones could explore Florence and all this countryside, which is very nice. They'd like it—but you would probably rather be cooler and quite free from housekeeping.

The Brett has gone back to the ranch, and is frantic because we don't go too. Mabel also writes urgingly. She has built two or three more houses and keeps one for us. But this summer anyhow we shan't go. I should like to see Bavaria again: and September should be lovely. If we went there any earlier, we would stay at that inn in Beurberg, where we began our career, at the end of May, fifteen years ago. I liked Beurberg so much. But now in summer I suppose the inn is crammed full.

I had notice from Curtis Brown today they had received ten pounds for "The Woman Who Rode Away." As soon as it appears, in the "Dial" or the "London Mercury," either in the June number or the July, I forget—I'll send you "The Man Who Loved Islands." I believe you'd like that, and it might amuse you to translate.

Well, it's not often I write such a long letter, nowadays. The days go by, and we hardly see anybody—which is what I prefer. Frieda grumbles sometimes, but when people come she doesn't want them. She has an idea she is a social soul who loves her fellowmen to distraction. I don't see it quite. But I suppose one idea of one's self is as good as another.

Remember me to the children, and to Alfred—and tante belle cose.

D. H. L.

Villa Mirenda
Scandicci
Florence
11 July 1927

My dear Mother-in-Law:

Your son-in-law is a poor wretch and is in bed again with bronchitis and hæmorrhage. We have the best doctor in Florence, Giglioli—he gives me coagulin but I am still in the corner. It is not dangerous, but . . . but . . .

And you, how are you? You are not taking any sea-baths? The doctor says my hæmorrhage comes from sea-bathing that I took in Forte.

And does it amuse you, your Konstanz? We were there at the Walthaus Jakob for supper, the time Mountsier was with us, do you remember? It was lovely. But aren't you a little lost and homeless there? Or are you always getting younger and are you shingling your hair and cutting your skirt short? You can never know what a woman will do in her green seventy-sixth year.

Friends are very good. Every day somebody comes from Florence. I've been only five days in bed and in a fortnight I can go away to that Wörtersee, but we don't know where it is yet—Emil should write. The doctor says I ought to go into the pines —eight hundred metres, no higher.

If only once I were well again!

I send you only two pounds for your birthday, since I am to bring the rest myself when we come for the feast. Else must write to us. Many thanks to her for her letters. I borrowed the book in London. But the Etruscan and all work can sleep with the devil, if only I get well again. I will enjoy myself and forget everything. You, be content, and take the joys of this earth peacefully.

We are coming soon and will eat the Baden sausages together.

D. H. L.

(Translated from the German)

IRSCHENHAUSEN
POST EBENHAUSEN
MUNICH
12 SEPTEMBER 1927

My Dear Mother-in-Law:

We had the little parcel today. But why did you spend so much money? You ought not to do it. The handkerchiefs are really charming. I like them very much, and the pralines are for princes, we've only eaten two rows. Good there was also a little sausage—bread is the staff of life but with a little sausage it also becomes an umbrella.

You are lonely, I know it, quite forlorn, with three daughters running all over the world. But now you'll be content again, Nusch is with you.

Else went this morning to sleep in Augsburg—God knows why—but we were very happy together, what with "patience" and embroidery and walks—what a pity she is gone!

The weather is cold and it rains—Nusch's barometer still makes a bad, grinning foreboding face in the room. But in the Isartal still hangs a gay-coloured rag of rainbow, the Lord still keeps his promise.

We haven't heard from Barby—I think she will come here direct, perhaps Saturday. Emil writes so nicely and sends me thirty bottles of malt-beer. Think what drunkards we shall become, arriving in Baden with red noses and watery eyes.

It is really a pity we can't stay together longer, with Nusch and Else and you. Always this stupid going away. But soon we shall see you, so farewell.

D. H. L.

It is evening, the clouds are gold, the mountains stand there with slow white pillows of steam.

(Translated from the German)

SATURDAY MORNING

Dear Else:

So nice of you to send all those toilet things, and the money—but why didn't you keep the money to pay for them? Let me know how much they cost.

The "Jugend" man came—a nice little soul after all—but they'll do him in—he'll never stand the modern mill. And the Kahlers came—both very nice—but like all people of that class nowadays, they have lost their raison d'être, and there seems no reason whatever why they should exist—they haven't even, like the Nachbarin, the poignancy of woes.

A rainy morning and a cold wind.

Barby arrives in München at 10:40 tonight—so Frieda will go in by a late train, and they'll come out tomorrow morning. We've promised to go to the Kahlers' tomorrow to tea.

Did you get the book I sent?—The "Jugend" man wants only a short—short story—four Schreibmaschineseiten: that's about two thousand words. No stories are as short as that—usually five thousand. I must try and hunt something up.

Hope all is well in Heidelberg. Greet everybody.

D. H. L.

This swanky paper comes from Fr. Häuselmaier—or however she is called.

IRSCHENHAUSEN
ISARTAL
WEDNESDAY
29 SEPTEMBER 1927

My dear Mother-in-Law:

Else writes Nusch is still there. Na, Johanna, you Easter-lamb, don't you sacrifice yourself yet on the altar of marriage. Wait then till Tuesday, when we are coming. We take the twelve o'clock train and arrive at seven in Baden, is that right, mother-in-law? And we go to the Augustabad, where the Blaufelchen is so good. It has turned much colder tonight—we've both had colds. Sunday was a horror of darkness and rain but we went out and got wet. But we are better. Anna is here and looks after us well. Barby is already in London. I can hardly believe she has been here. I've nearly drunk all the beer Emil sent, a record for Munich, no? Yesterday we went to see Frau Leitner, so nice and small, but what chatter. She sends you all her greetings.

The beeches begin to turn yellow and today we gathered some violets under the balcony—they smell sweet like spring and the flowers are still wonderful. Kahlers come tomorrow and Max Mohr, the dramatist, is to come from Tegernsee. Then, you, mother-in-law, and I hope you too, Nusch—will meet us on Tuesday and everything can be told then.

D. H. L.

(Translated from the German)

HOTEL EDEN
BADEN-BADEN
FRIDAY

My dear Else:

You also have a birthday, but it seems to me one must be four or eighty to have important birthdays. Of the number we won't speak.

I had your letter. Yes, we saw Hans Carossa, a nice man, mild like mashed potatoes. He listened to my lung passages, he could not hear my lungs, thinks they must be healed, only the bronchi, and doctors are not interested in bronchi. But he says not to take more inhalations with hot air: it might bring the hæmorrhage back. The journey was vile, many people, much dust, and I had a cold. But it is better. We are very grand here, two rooms, a bath, and the food very good.

Yesterday it was goose, Michaelmas goose; I can eat better but they bring so much, wagonloads of potatoes, and cutlets big as carpets, and how the people feed! It takes my shy appetite away a bit.

The mother-in-law grows younger and younger. We must go back like this on her next birthday: 66 next time, then 55 years. It is thus with old age, the only real youth without trouble, after seventy.

Max Mohr came in a car from Tegernsee, where he has a pleasant house—with wife and child—a man thirty-six years old or so.

He wants to be a child of nature but we were disappointed in the nature. But he is good and interesting, but a last man who has arrived at the last end of the road, who can no longer go ahead in the wilderness nor take a step into the unknown. So he is very unhappy, is a doctor, prisoner of war in England, and his psychology a little like Hadu's. We have his plays, we send them to you.

When are you coming? Come this weekend. We stay till the seventeenth. We are very fortunate here, but the world seems dark to me again. That scares me and I want to go south.

I send you the story—too long for "Jugend"—but you might sell it somewhere else. Would not "Tickets Please" and "England, My England" be just right for "Jugend"? Have you got them? The piece about the dog I can't find. But come and we can talk it all over. Are Friedel and Marianne there? Greet Alfred and them.

D. H. L.

(Translated from the German)

VILLA MIRENDA
SCANDICCI
FIRENZE
14 NOVEMBER 1927

Dear Else:

Many thanks for the Beethoven letters—arrived today—not a literary man—and always in love with somebody—or thought *he was—and in the flesh wasn't. But how German! —I mean the way he really* wasn't.

Frau Katherina Kippenberg wrote they want to publish one of my books next year, and asks which I would suggest. I think I shall suggest, "Woman Who Rode Away," and "The Princess" (from the English "St. Mawr") and a third story you haven't yet seen, "None of That." They'd make a smallish volume. Or would you suggest one of the novels? "The Lost Girl" or "Aaron's Rod." I don't care. Only we'll keep back "The Plumed Serpent," and offer it ready translated *to another firm, for 1929. Do you think that's wise?*

It has rained a bit here, but is sunny again—we're just going out for a walk—the country is full of colour, vines yellow, olives blue, pines very green. It is Monday, so the fusillade of cacciatori shooting little birds is quieter—it makes me so mad— I am really quite a lot better—cough much less, especially in the morning—but haven't yet been to Firenze—think we'll go Thursday. There's a queer sort of unease in the air—as if the wrong sort of spirits were flying abroad in the unseen ether— but it may be my imagination. Frieda strums away on her piano, and I have to listen for when she hits a wrong note.—I am dabbing at poems, getting them ready for the "Collected Poems."

Alfred wrote very nicely from Ascona. I hope we'll see you here in the early spring: if we are here: I feel sort of uncertain and unstuck. I hope you're having more conferences and so on, if they amuse you. As for me, I play "patience"—and it hardly ever comes out. Love!

D. H. L.

VILLA MIRENDA
SCANDICCI
FLORENCE
16 NOVEMBER 1927

My dear Mother-in-Law:

This time I want you to do something for me: our neighbour at the ranch, Rachel Hawk, wants toys for the children. She wants two boxes—a farmyard and a village, not too small, to cost five marks. The people in the shop can send it direct: Mrs. Rachel Hawk, Del Monte Ranch, Questa, New Mexico. And in the shop buy also animals and trees and men, as small as possible, also chickens, and little houses and carts and so forth for my niece Joan and my nephew Bertie, for about ten marks. They can be sent straight from the shop to my sister Emily.

I send you two pounds, that will be enough. You like doing it, yes? In the shop on the Augustplatz, where the large autos stand.

How are you? We are well. It has turned cold, but sun all day today. I was on the top of the hill, I saw Florence, lying there in the sunshine, so light and clear, the lilytown.

Tomorrow we are going for lunch with Reggie; the first time I shall go to town since we came back. If it is fine like today I'll go with pleasure.

We are both busy—I am writing stories and am typing all my poems, they are to be collected in one volume. Frieda has finished her jacket, very pretty, from the violet velvet Nusch gave her. It is really pretty, a short jacket with silver buttons, quite Florentine Renaissance.

In the evening we have a fire in the stove. The day is warm, the sun streams into the room. But the evenings are cold.

Max Mohr writes always very nicely and will come to see us in January. Perhaps we shall go to Cortina, we are not going to Egypt. But if we both keep well, we shall stay in our own house.

I always have a "patience" in the evening and I think the mother-in-law has a game at this same hour. Yours comes better than Else's. If your little one is called the demon, then Else's ought to be called "devil."

Else sent me Beethoven's letters. But what a cut-off man! He could not come near to anybody: and his house, what untidyness, what a mad show! The poor, great man! Thank the Lord, I am still small enough to mend my socks and wash my cup.

Frieda has written to you: the letter lies about these last two days, half finished. You will get it finally, when it arrives.

I greet you, mère éternelle! A pity we can't send you our roses. they are so lovely.

D. H. L.

(Translated from the German)

VILLA MIRENDA
SCANDICCI
FIRENZE
12 DECEMBER 1927

Dear Else:

I can't help laughing at the end of Frau Katherina's letter—gets quite snappy. However, that's that. I suppose by "Holy Ghosts" (imagine daring to pluralize it!) she means "Glad Ghosts." I sent you a copy last year—didn't I?—little yellow book. I don't mind what they put in a volume.—I suggested "Woman Who Rode Away" and "Princess" and "None of That"—all more or less Mexican. But let her put in "Glad Ghosts" if she likes. Anyhow we have got her hipped. Don't suddenly go and say you don't want to translate the things—or haven't time, or something—just when I've got it into order. It would be just like you.

Very grey and misty and unsatisfactory here. I am in bed, as the best place out of it all. But I'm all right—cough a nuisance still, but nothing extra. I'd get up if the sun would shine. Anyhow I'll get up this afternoon.

I'm writing my "Lady Chatterley" novel over again. It's very "shocking"—the Schwiegermutter must never see it.—I think I shall publish it privately here in Florence.

We are staying here for Christmas and making a tree for the peasants. This year there'll be at least thirty of them. Dreadful thought. But Frieda wants it.

And we aren't sending out any Christmas presents—so

LAWRENCE AND ALDOUS HUXLEY

please, Else, don't send us anything. The post is so tiresome here, and altogether one feels so unchristmassy. I'm sick of Jesus, and don't see at all why he should go on being born every year. We might have somebody else born, for a change. Toujours perdrix!

The Huxleys will be in Florence for Christmas, then going to Diablerets. I don't want to go there, another San Moritz, where Michael Arlen has gone. I'd have liked to go to Egypt, but the fates seem to say no. So it's just San Polo!

The Schwiegermutter says you are having festas in Heidelberg, so I suppose you are wearing your best clothes and going it. Nothing like learning, for setting people on the hop.

Anyhow I hope you're having a good time, and the children too.

Love from both.

D. H. L.

VILLA MIRENDA
SCANDICCI
FLORENCE
SUNDAY

My dear Mother-in-Law:

Christmas is here again. I say, the poor chap has been born nearly two thousand times, it is enough. He might really have peace now, and leave us in peace, without Christmas and stomach-aches. But we sit still and only make the tree for the peasant children and they think it is a miracle, that it really grows here in the salon, and has silver apples and golden birds: for them it is only a fairytale, nothing Christian. You've heard how Frieda wanted to act Sancta Sanctissima, she's really St. Frieda, butter doesn't melt in her mouth: because, of course, she has taken a Bandelli child to the hospital. But, thank the Lord, the child makes trouble and Saint Frieda begins to be bored and is becoming all-too-human again.

The Wilkinsons, our neighbours, have just been here, he with a flute and an overcoat. Tomorrow they go to Rome for a fortnight. Thank goodness I'm not going: there is an ice-cold wind these last two days and Rome is an ice-cold town.

I sit here in the corner by the stove that sings quite amiably and the world can go to blazes as far as I am concerned.

Else wrote that she will take you to Heidelberg over the holidays. But don't you go, remain safely there, and let the mistletoe berries fall on those that want them.

The Wilkinsons have brought me a Christmas pudding: it

smells good; I'll enjoy it. I send you a pound, you can buy such a one—yes, a real English pudding. (Don't!)

Then farewell. Don't drink too much and dance too much and flirt too much, or you'll have a real moral "morning-after," and I shan't weep with you.

Farewell, O Germania under the tree.

D. H. L.

(Translated from the German)

VILLA MIRENDA
SCANDICCI
WEDNESDAY

My dear Mother-in-Law:

Lo, everything is nearly normal again. The tree is still standing—we want to relight it when the Wilkes return from Rome, perhaps Monday. And we have the remains of the plum pudding from yesterday. Otherwise, as I say, we are nearly normal. Frieda has forgotten her holiness for the moment. The boy flew away from the hospital, his padrone took him back again and promised him a bicycle. So, the operation is done, Frieda is going to visit him tomorrow. But now she is no longer the one and only saint. The padrone promised Dino a bicycle and Dante, the elder brother, says: "If somebody promises me a bicycle I'll also go and be operated on." But, poor boy, he has no rupture.

The weather is abominable—rain and little sun—evening is the best time, with fire and lamp and peace. Frieda is making herself an apron all covered with roses and birds.

The tie is a great success. I wore it on Christmas day in Florence—very nice, it's much nicer on than off. The Baden calendar lies faithfully here, ready to carry us through another year, with all the pictures. The last sheet of the old one hangs over the piano, a black and white scene in the Black Forest.

Oh, dear mother-in-law, live well for another year and have a jolly, happy 1928. Greet Else, I am writing to her.

Your, D. H. L.

The book from Friedel is pretty, really pretty.

(Translated from the German)

VILLA MIRENDA
SCANDICCI
FLORENCE
WEDNESDAY

My dear Mother-in-Law:

I haven't said "thank you" yet for the beautiful tie that I like so much. I'm a brute. But now the pen has become a difficulty to me. I have written so much in my life, I would like to be silent. But you understand.

We are well on in January and I haven't had a cold yet this winter. I thank the Lord and pray it may go on so with me. You are also well, aren't you?

We are sitting still and work much, and that's healthy. People make you tired and bring sickness. Frieda is sewing much, makes herself some dresses and jackets and a coat, and says she is better than Paquin. All right! Her hats grow higher and higher, like the tower of Babel, which was so high. In the spring you'll see a daughter such as you've never seen before in all your life.

Now they write to me from London that "David" won't be produced until April. I prefer it, I would rather go to England or Germany when the winter is past and the flowers greet you. Wait a little, mother-in-law, have a little patience, summer is the best time. We are having bad weather, not rain but cold fog that is quite unnatural in this country. But beautiful days in between: like Monday, when I went to the Villa Curonia, Mabel's villa on the Poggio Imperiale, for the first time. Oh dear, a big, beautiful villa, somewhat noble, but sad, sad as death. She wants to pull out some books and send them to Taos. Farewell, mother-in-law, till we meet.

D. H. L.

(Translated from the German)

VILLA MIRENDA
SCANDICCI
FLORENCE
SUNDAY

My dear Mother-in-Law:

I have the ties, they are beautiful as Rhinegold, but why "for rainy days"? Today I am wearing the blue and red, do you remember? I believe it is only cotton, but you ought to see how gay and manly it looks. We are still waiting for my novel, "Lady Chatterley's Lover." Only half has been printed—all goes slowly. But I hope in a fortnight it will be ready—at least printed.

It's just as well we aren't in Switzerland yet, the wind comes cold and the snow lies deep on the hills opposite. Today was a wonderful day but no warmer than a sunny winter's day. I don't want to be in the snow again, as at Diablerets. We are looking for an inn in Switzerland. In the hotels sit thousands of English spinsters and they bore me. In an inn, life is more natural. Barby writes there is a good inn at Talloire, near Annecy where Nusch was, but it is in Switzerland. Ask Nusch about it. Frieda can go to Baden when she likes, but I think it would be stupid for only five or six days and then off again. What a pity we can't both come while Nusch is there! But for me everybody says: "Switzerland! Switzerland!"—so I, poor beast, have to go. But later in the summer I'm coming to Baden.

Frieda is still sewing clothes. The two girls, Giulia and Teresina, come in the evenings and the three sew and talk to-

gether in the dining-room, but I sit alone here in the salotto, too many females for me.

The spring vegetables are here already—asparagus, sweet young peas, broad beans, and during the last three weeks new potatoes and many artichokes. It is always a good moment in Italy when the vegetables come. For fruit we have nespole, the yellow Japanese misplein, and the first cherries, which are not really sweet. Everything is late this year and many, many roses but not happy ones. They fall off in a day because the undersoil is still too dry, the rain has not yet gone deep down.

You remember Zaira, the mistress of the major here, and the big white dog Titi? Well, Titi has bitten Zaira's arm badly and has had to be shot, and poor Zaira must stay at home, there in Florence, till the doctor is sure that it isn't hydrophobia. Frieda says: another of my enemies fallen—she means Titi.

Poor A . . . H . . .—she was so nice but seemed so small and lost here in Italy. And poor Frau H . . .—really ill. I hope they are all right again in Baden. Don't you go travelling to Spain or Sweden, mother-in-law—old ladies should stay in their own home-town. Then farewell to you two—we'll meet again before long.

D. H. L.

(Translated from the German)

Villa Mirenda
Scandicci
Florence
Thursday

My dear Mother-in-Law:

We had a good journey, few people, no difficulties, and I was not very tired. I never saw Switzerland so lovely: a still grey autumn day, grass so strangely green, nearly like fire; and then the fruit trees, all delicate flames, the cherry trees absolutely red like cherries, apple trees and pear trees yellow red scarlet and still as flowers: really like a fairyland. It has rained in Italy. But today there is gentle sun and clouds, warm air and a great stillness. The neighbours were at the station with the car, all so friendly. And here the peasants all ranged on the "aia"—Giulia radiant, she is getting quite pretty; she had the fires ready and hot water and we are here. But the house seemed foreign to me, naked and empty, and a bit uncanny, as if I had never known it, but Frieda is happy.

I don't know what it is with me, I don't feel at home in Italy, this time. In your little vase are roses and jasmine. My pictures please me—and I listen, listen to the stillness. But now we go to the neighbours. Take our small presents. Already your letter was here this morning. What a pity that distance remains distance, so absolutely. If we could come for tea to you, we would all three be happy. But we will come nearer to live, near you.

Auf Wiedersehen, be happy. D. H. L.

(Translated from the German)

VILLA MIRENDA
SCANDICCI
FLORENCE
MONDAY

My dear Mother-in-Law:

I am glad you had such a beautiful trip to Herrenalp. Are you glad to come home or would you have liked to stay longer?

We arrive about the thirteenth. We leave next Monday the twelfth for Milan, and on Tuesday the thirteenth from Milan to Baden-Baden. We arrive at 6:45 in the evening. Can you find us one or two rooms in a villa or a hotel, that we can eat where we want to? And then, after a few days, we can go again to Herrenalp with you, or stay in Baden or somewhere in the neighbourhood.

We promised to be in England all the month of August. But that leaves us about twenty days in Germany. It will be lovely.

I am always fond of Baden and the Black Forest, and always feel well there. It will be splendid summer, and the strawberries and cherries won't be over yet.

We can eat at the Wald Kaffee, drink tea there, and visit Excellenz Stötzer in her wooden house and make excursions. Yes, it will be lovely. Frieda also is happy to come, really. Don't be sad.

It is wonderful here, so warm and still. The fruit is already ripe: figs, peaches, apricots, plums, all big and fine, because it rained so much—the apricots are marvellous, really as big as peaches, and the first little pears are so sweet and pale yellow. Yes, it is full summer.

My sisters write sadly because of the strike: there is no end to it and both are losing much money. One must not make one's life out of money, if money disappears the life is broken. With or without money I have had my life for myself and am not swindled.

Friedel wrote nicely from Berlin but I think he has had enough of a big town and wants to go home.

Else must tell me how she likes the play.

They are already translating "The Plumed Serpent" into Swedish but I only get six hundred marks.

I send you a little money for your birthday, tnat you may buy what you like.

We won't bring you any presents, they are such a nuisance.

Then, mother-in-law, soon we'll meet.

D. H. L.

(Translated from the German)

VILLA MIRENDA
SCANDICCI
FLORENCE
SUNDAY

My dear Mother-in-Law:

This is already another Sunday, and the third that we are here. The weather is always like summer, so warm and clear, the windows are open all day and we don't dream of having a fire: the evenings also are quite warm. The roses are in bloom, but there are few flowers, all is still too dry, little water even in the wells. Also Baden will be lovely just now. On Sundays I must always think of the music in the "Kurpark" and of the "Malzbier" in your room. Here there is no music, the stupid hunters shoot the sparrows and nightingales in the woods behind, you always hear it go "pop"—Malzbier there isn't either, and your room is not just five minutes from here. But you will be going for a walk at this moment and you will be meeting all the ladies from the Stift in their Sunday clothes returning from Mass.

Nusch has written—says she sees many people, and goes out a lot. She wants to come here in March. Alfred also has written from Ascona—quite charmed by the paradisial days there: a charming letter. Frieda has a piano again, now she wants to play Händel, the "Messiah," but she hasn't arrived at the Alleluia! I am painting a picture, not very big, of a tiger who springs on a man: such a grinning tiger. Tomorrow we are going to Florence with friends. I haven't been to town yet. We play cards with the neighbours, solo-whist and Pope John and also "patience." You know, your little "patience"—the one-two-three—the one that is called the demon, may well be called so, with me it never comes right.

Greet Frau Kugler, also the Halms. I hope that Frau Oberin is better. You keep jolly; you must ask the cards if in January we are going to Cortina. "O dear cards, tell me truly . . ."

D. H. L.

LES DIABLERETS
THURSDAY MORNING

[To Frieda]

No letter from you this morning—only one letter from Curtis Brown, asking for the "Lady C." MS.—But I am still waiting for the final two chapters from that woman.

A warm morning, with warm dimmish sun. Our maid got the grippe, so her sister is here.

I'm just going down to the station with Aldous. Diablerets coming to an end for us. I do hope we shan't get gripped going down to the valley.—How do you feel it?

Love to die Alte.

D. H. L.

CHALET BEAU SITE
LES DIABLERETS
VAUD
TUESDAY

Dear Else:

We'll just go ahead with "Rex" without bothering about Curtis Brown. I'll just mention it to him when I write, and tell him I fixed things up myself. I think M. 180 is quite a good price for "Jugend" to pay: and the usual arrangement is one third to the translator, two thirds to the author—so you get M. 60. Business, cara mia, business!

I wrote Secker direct and asked him to send you and to Frau Katherina both, copies of the "Princess" (in "St. Mawr") and proofs of the volume of short stories "The Woman Who Rode Away." I hope you will get these directly. In the stories, the end of "The Border Line" is missing—printer lost two or three pages: so I'm having to write it in. But you'll understand the story is unfinished. It's "None of That" I want you to consider.

We had hot sunshine, and the snow was melting: but now today it is snowing again, a fine and crumbling snow. I must say, I don't like it. I am no snow-bird, I hate the stark and shroudy whiteness, white and black. It offends the painter in one—it is so uniform—only sometimes lovely contours, and pale blue gleams. But against life.

I've been busy doing my poems—have at last got all the early poems together and complete. What a sweat! But I shall pub-

lish the others, "Look!" and "Birds and Beasts" as they stand. Then I'll have to go through the novel, which I'm having typed in London. How glad I'll be when all this work is behind me, and I needn't give a damn any more. I'm sick to death of literature.

I think this place is a good tonic, but snow isn't good for bronchials: it just isn't: it scrapes inside.

I dreamt of Frau v. Kahler last night. Are they all right? That was such a good p.c. of Irschenhausen.

F. waiting to take the letter—so Wiedersehen!

D. H. L.

FIRENZE
16 APRIL 28
SATURDAY

[To Else]

Had your note from Alassio—glad you liked it there. I wonder if you are setting off today for Germany. I stayed the night in Florence at Orioli's, but came back to Mirenda this afternoon. There is an atmosphere of departure and departure, which is a bit écoeurant. I wish we were safely away, with no good-byes to say.—We shall meet some time during the summer somewhere nice and free and forgetful. Italy has too many memories, not enough spunk.

I shall send your Füllfeder, which I just discovered.

D. H. L.

VILLA MIRENDA
SCANDICCI
FLORENCE
4 MAY 1928

Dear Else:

I simply can't write biographical facts about myself. Will you answer this Bülow man, if you feel like it: and if you think it is worth while. I have never heard of him. I must ask Curtis Brown if they have arranged with him about "Islands."

You have heard by now that we are keeping on the Mirenda. I took down the pictures and we began to pack: but Frieda became so gloomy that I hung the pictures up again and paid six months' rent. Not worth while getting into a state about. So here we are, just the same. And probably we shall stay till the end of the month, as the proofs of the novel are still *only half done. I wish the printer would hurry up.*

I am asking people if they know of a nice Gasthaus in Switzerland, for me. I hate hotel-pensions, after a few days. I always want to kill the old women—usually English—that come into meals like cats. We just had a very handsome Louis XV sort of a one to tea—but American this time—and of course I'm bristling in every hair.

It is more or less summer too—the Kastanien in full flower—is yours too? The Bandelli peasants just brought us the first baccelli—Saubohnen—which are tiny, and they eat them raw, and think them wonderful. I like them because il baccello is one of the improper words. We also eat green almonds boiled in sugar and water, like plums—and they taste like gooseberries. We went to see an old Englishwoman—not so very old—who has a very elegant flat on the Lungarno and was a cocotte—the expensive sort—but a real one. I must say, I find her very restful and smooth, after some of the others.

Au revoir—tante cosa!

D. H. L.

VILLA MIRENDA
SCANDICCI
FIRENZE
FRIDAY

Dear Else:

I will send this to Baden—perhaps you will still be there. You will have had a lovely sunny week: here the sun is too hot, makes one tired, and feels like earthquakes. Still, it is beautiful.

We got home safely with all the spoil—there are roses in the Wolfratshauser glass you gave me, here on the table—and we drank the Kirsch from the little yellow glasses when the Wilkinsons were here yesterday. I am much better, I eat more joyfully, and take the Brustthee. Imagine, one must let it boil slowly for hours. I do believe it is good, better than all the medicines. I am already doing a story, and dabbing at my picture of five Negresses—called "The Finding of Moses," or, if the Schwiegermutter had to name it, "ein fürchterliches Schauerstück." À la bonne heure.

I had a letter from Curtis Brown, saying that next year, in November, our contract with Kippenberg comes to an end, and then we can leave him and go to a different publisher. Also that he, Kip, said in a letter of 1923 that he would gladly agree that you should do the translations. Curtis Brown's have the letter. Now I have written Kippenberg to ask him what exactly he intends to do next year, with regard to my work. We'll see if we can't have our own way in this matter, and you shall translate "The Plumed Serpent," if you wish, trotz Anton, trotz Katherina. Vogue la galère!

Dark falling. We haven't made any fire in the stove yet—it is so warm. Hope you are feeling well and easy. Love to the Schwiegermutter—the Schlips came today—but I shan't wear it yet. Say thanks for me.

Love,

D. H. L.

VILLA MIRENDA
SCANDICCI
FIRENZE
MONTAG

Liebe Else:

You wrote me so nicely from Constance.—I'm glad you had a good time with the Schwiegermutter. I can so well understand she didn't want to see her old home. It's too upsetting: the past is so far off.

I am better—getting up again, and going about the house—but feeling feeble. I went downstairs and out of doors a few yards yesterday—but it's too hot to go out till sundown. However, this day week—or tomorrow week—I hope we can leave for Villach. I shall feel better a little higher. It's lovely weather here, sunny, and not too hot at all if one keeps quiet. But it's much too hot to walk in the sun. If I was well, I should enjoy it. Frieda for the first time really likes the heat. But now I feel I should like to see the world green, and hear the waters running: and to taste good northern food.

I almost wish we'd arranged with you to rent Irschenhausen for August too, and gone straight there. But it will be nice to see Nusch too—and as you say, if one can really be amused, that is the chief thing. My illnesses I know come from chagrin—chagrin that goes deep in and comes out afterwards in hæmorrhage *or what not. When one learns, also, not to be chagrined, then one can become like your Bürgermeister—was he a Bürgermeister?—fat and lustig, to the age of eighty. Anyhow I'd be glad to be fat and lustig once before I die: even a bit versoffen, if that's a way of not having a sore chest.*

I wonder if the "revolution" in Vienna, which the papers report, amounts to anything? Probably not. I think if we didn't go to Austria we'd go to Bavaria, or somewhere high in Baden.

We shall see you then in September. It is good of you to let us have the Irschenhausen house—but I must pay you a rent.

Wiedersehen!

D. H. L.

I sent you a "Dial" with a story in it—don't know if you'll like it.

Kesselmatte
Gsteig b Gstaad
Schweiz
11 September 1928

My dear Mother-in-Law:

I have your letter and the tie, a nice one. Yes, we're coming soon. Else comes here Saturday the fifteenth and stays till Sunday.

It's wonderfully still here since my sister and niece went. They left Friday. They were jolly here but my sister is a little sad—the husband is nothing.

We have had summer days but today is autumn. The clouds turn round and round the tops of the mountains, still and grey and low, so still it is frightening. In these mountains one needs the sun. It will be nice in Baden, when the Brewsters are also there and we can go to concerts and theatres together.

We eat pounds of grapes. Frieda makes a diet of grapes, juniper berries, and God knows what. Do you hear nothing from Nusch? Farewell and soon,

Auf Wiedersehen,

D. H. L.

(Translated from the German)

La Vigie
Île de Port-Cros
Var
Saturday

Dear Else:

Your letter today, saying the Schwiegermutter is in bed. I'm awfully sorry and do hope it's not much. I thought in Lichtental she wasn't well. Of course, she is a heavy woman, and her legs are sure to suffer. Let us know how she goes on—and I hope she'll soon be up and about.

We are here settled in. But Frieda arrived in Lavandou with that fatal Italian Grippe, and of course I took it. I felt ill all last week, and have been in bed all this, with a very raked chest. Sickening!—The others are very nice and very kind. The Vigie isn't a castle at all—just a low thick defence-wall with loop-holes, enclosing the top of the hill—about as big as the Leopoldpatz—and the inside all wild, grown with lavender and arbutus and little pine trees, and with a few rooms built against the inside of the wall. It's quite pleasant, and comfortable, and we have big fires of pine logs in the open fires. Giuseppe is a strong fellow of twenty-eight, Sicilian. He fetches and carries and washes all dishes and makes fires. The women only cook, and they do it in turns. Joseph brings the food from the boat on a small donkey, Jasper—and we get abundance. The ship comes nearly every day—but the post only three times a week. The climate is very warm—warm and moist. I am afraid that doesn't suit me very well. I don't know how long we shall stay. I have promised, till December 15 or 20. But if the warm-moist is bad for my cough, we shall leave soon. The others are really very nice and kind, it will be a pity if we have to leave them. And where shall we go?

The Brewsters are back in Capri. Inevitable.

I ordered the poems to Heidelberg. They look very nice.

We are on the top of the island, and look down on green pine-tops, down to the blue sea, and the other islands and the mainland. Since I came I have not been down to the sea again—and Frieda has bathed only once. But it is very pretty. And at night the lights flash at Toulon and Hyères and Lavandou.—But I really don't like islands, I would never stay long on one. Frieda wants to go back to Lago di Garda. Vediamo! I am in abeyance.

Write and tell us how the Schwiegermutter is. Frieda says she feels worried—but it seems to me there is no danger, only it is painful and depressing. No peace on this earth.

Love from both.

D. H. L.

I hope this letter will leave the island before next Tuesday—the next mail.

PORT-CROS
FRIDAY

Such storms, such wind, such torrents of rain! And the Vigie, although quite hygienic, *is not very* comfortable. *So we are all leaving next week—Tuesday or Thursday, as the sea permits. I think Frieda and I will stay in Bandol, on the big railway.*

Am so glad the Schwiegermutter is better.

Will write next week.

D. H. L.

ÎLE DE PORT-CROS
VAR
WEDNESDAY

My dear Mother-in-Law:

I am glad you are better. You have been too brave. You know, you are heavy on your feet now, you are no longer a young, light thing. You must not walk so far. I remember with grief the "Fisch Kultur" a mad excursion and you insisted doing it. No, no, you must go gently and wisely. To force things is not for you.

Tomorrow we leave here. Thank the Lord, the weather is good, blue sky, blue quiet sea, and so warm. But I have enough. I would never like to stay more than a month on a little island. But as an experience it was nice. I think we will only go as far as Bandol, a little place on the coast, half an hour from Toulon. But there we are on the main line, and only an hour from Marseille. And we can think where we really want a house—neither of us knows what we want.

They write from Florence it rains and rains and rains; awful. Thank God, we aren't there. My book of stories came with the Inselalmanach and Möricke. You know I have not broken with Insel? They pay me fifty pounds instead of thirty-five and Else can translate when she wants to. That's good.

I send you five pounds, if you want more tell me. It is my money and I give it you with pleasure, but please pay the ten marks for Frieda's dress.

The Brewsters are in Capri again. They say it is the best place in the world. Good, when you know it!

Keep still and quiet inside yourself, then your legs will go without pain.

D. H. L.

(Translated from the German)

Hôtel Beau Rivage
Bandol, Var
19 December 1928

My dear Mother-in-Law:

This evening the ties and the calendar came. The friendly calendar, we know it so well, it makes me homesick. We must really find a house, if it is only to hang it on the wall. But we still don't know where we want to live. It is very nice here, so sunny and friendly. Now we wait till Xmas is past.

Perhaps Else and Barby are coming. Tomorrow we shall know. But Else is working till the end of February, so she can only stay a week. She says she wants to come before she gets married; because really she wants to get married at last. Barby is not very well. Perhaps she will stay some weeks with us.

We have a friend here, a young writer, quite nice and faithful. First Frieda did not like him because he's not beautiful—but now she thinks him quite good-looking and she likes him. We also had a young Australian here for two days, this afternoon he left for Nice. He makes those beautiful expensive books that people collect nowadays—he says he will make a book next year of my paintings—of all my paintings, with a foreword by me, to be sold at ten guineas each. It seems madness to me, but it's his money and he will pay me well—if he does it. But how mad people are—there is quite a large vogue in editions de luxe that cost two or five or even twenty-five pounds. I hate it.

Rhys Davies, the friend who is here, is Welsh and his grandfather was also a miner.

Max Mohr writes a little sadly from his "Wolfgrube," he says he must always fight with his editors and has little money. There in Bavaria the snow is deep.

I am glad that you are better. I also feel better, but hot sun and cold wind find my bronchi, that feel a bit raw. It is always so in weather like this.

Else will be there, with you—she will give you five pounds from me, from "Jugend," and keeps the rest. You will have a quiet, good, happy Xmas, only keep still inside yourself.

Greet them all from me. And Nusch? She won't be there any more. I will write her and Emil. I hope we shall see them this spring, here on the Mediterranean, where the sun is so bright, and the sea so blue, and the small boats so white and dancing. Very friendly I find also the Frenchmen, they leave you alone and don't hang on so heavily. But Frieda is always longing for Italy, I think.

So farewell, mother-in-law. Merry Xmas. What flowers have you? Here are many narcissi in the fields. Merry Xmas! Merry Xmas!

D. H. L.

(Translated from the German)

Hotel Príncipe Alfonso
Palma de Mallorca
Spain
12 June 1929

Dear Else:

We want to leave here next Tuesday—eighteenth—by the boat to Marseille. Frieda sprained her ankle, bathing, but I think it will be better by then—it's not bad. I want her to go and see after my pictures, as the show is supposed to open this week. And the book is ready today—I have a set of the coloured plates—twenty-six—rather good, although only done in three-colour process. I hear they have already orders for about three hundred copies at ten guineas, and ten vellum copies at fifty guineas are all ordered. World of crazes! But I ought to make about five hundred pounds out of the book—not bad. I shan't send you a copy—I know you don't care especially about it—and in these things you belong to the opposite direction, so of course you don't see much value in work of this sort. You say satanisch. *Perhaps you are right; Lucifer is brighter now than tarnished Michael or shabby Gabriel. All things fall in their turn, now Michael goes down, and whispering Gabriel, and the Son of the Morning will laugh at them all. Yes, I am all for Lucifer, who is really the Morning Star. The real principle of Evil is not anti-Christ or anti-Jehovah, but anti-life. I agree with you in a sense, that I am with the anti-Christ. Only I am not anti-life.*

If Frieda comes to England from Marseille, I shall probably go to North Italy, the Garda, where it won't be too hot. This year I don't want to come very far north—I feel I am better south of the Alps—really. Probably, Frieda will come to Baden on her way back from England.

This island is a queer place—so dry—but at last it has rained. We might possibly come back next winter.

I expect the Schwiegermutter will have gone back to the Stift. I was glad she was well enough to come to Heidelberg. It must be summer with you, leafy and lovely. Here it is all dried up, only the bushes of wild thyme in flower on the waste places, and the bougainvillæas in the gardens.

I wonder where you will go for the summer holiday? Anyhow we will meet somewhere, if not in Baden.

Greet everybody from me.

D. H. L.

6 Lungarno Corsini
Florence
Sunday
7 July

[To Frieda]

Maria drove me to Pisa yesterday afternoon—very sirocco and overcast, but not hot, not at all uncomfortable. Unfortunately my inside is upset—either I must have eaten something or it came from drinking ice-water very cold on Thursday when it was very hot. Anyhow my lower man hurts and it makes my chest sore—which is a pity, because I was so well. Now I'm rather limp. But I've kept still all day in Pino's flat, and he looks after me well—so I hope by tomorrow or Tuesday it will be all right. Luigino Franchetti said he'd got ptomaine poisoning, on Friday at Forte—but I think it was an upset too, nothing serious. I think mine is going off. Pino's flat gets a bit hot just at evening, but in the night and the most part of the day it is pleasant and cool—it's not really a hot year. Carletto has gone off for a day's tramp in the hills beyond Fiesole. Pino and I will have a cup of tea now, then perhaps take a carriage-drive for an hour.

I had your mother's letter this morning—she says you are all going up to Plässig or somewhere on the thirteenth—which is next Saturday. What is it like there? Probably I shall arrive in Baden by then—it depends a bit on the innards. I wanted to look at the Lake of Como to see if we'd like a house there—but am not sure if I shall want to make the effort. And I was so well before.

X . . . Y . . . is staying on in Forte, thank God—till about fifteenth. She must be in Paris by twenty-third—sails on twenty-seventh—thank heaven. She is a mixture of the worst side of Arabella—turns up her eyes in that awful indecent fashion—and of I . . . L . . .—humble, cringing, yet impudent, with an eternal and ceaseless self-preoccupation, tangled up in her own ego till it's shameful—thinking all and only of herself. Ugh, she's awful. At the same time, she's a poor pathetic thing. She has sent you a feather thing that she says is for a little cape—pretty—but I shall leave it behind in the trunk. I am leaving this trunk here also—the money they cost in transport and facchinaggio is awful, pure waste—and the bother.

Well, I've not had a coherent or sensible letter from you since you left Paris—so I suppose you were gone overhead—and then it's no use saying anything. However, emerge quickly—and we'll see if we can settle the problem of a house.

Had a letter from Barby—but it wasn't somehow very nice—same cattiveria as M . . ., underneath—or so it seemed. I suppose you didn't go and see my sisters. Hope Else is better. Aldous was very well, I've never seen him so well. Am seeing nobody here. No sound from Brett about MSS. or ranch. Think I shall come by night to Milano—but hate sharing a berth with some stranger. Hope you are nice and peaceful in Baden.

L.

I really think Italy is not good for my health—the country is much slacker, *all going deflated—and lots of poverty again, so they say. But everybody is very* nice, *much softer once more, and sort of subdued.*

FLORENCE
MONDAY NIGHT

[To Frieda]

The pains were a chill—have been in bed all day today—damn! Pino very nice, but oh the noise of traffic. I'm a lot better. I want to get up tomorrow, and leave if possible on Wednesday night for Milan. I might arrive Baden on Thursday night—otherwise Friday—all being well. Hot internal cold I've got, real Italian. I hate this country like poison, sure it would kill me.

I should rather like an apartment for six weeks or so—Ebersteinburg, Baden—anywhere—where I can lie in bed all day if I want to—and where I needn't see people. But don't at all know what you feel like, since you have not written lately.

Rained a bit today—quite cool. Pino and Carletto gone out into town.

D. H. L.

Shall wire—suppose you had all my letters addressed to the Kingsley.

Hotel Löwen
Lichtental
13 August 1929

Dear Else:

Hans says it rains in Bavaria, and Max Mohr says it rains in Bavaria, so I suppose it does. Only now I hope it has left off. Here it is quite decent, sunny mornings, cloudy afternoons, and quite pleasant. The Schwiegermutter is here, but says she will go back to the Stift on Thursday. On Friday her "heissgeliebte Anita" is due to arrive with the not so heissgeliebter-aberdochgeliebter Hinke: they will stay a while here in the Löwen. I have never met the Hinke, so I have a joy in store.

We had the 50n Geburtstagsfeier on Sunday evening, very noble, Bowle, trout, ducks, and nine people—three Halms, two Schweikhards, one Kugler—and they all seemed *very happy and we all kept it up very bravely. But alas, next day Frieda was in one of the worst moods I have ever seen her in!—a Seelenkater, or however you spell it.*

You hear the pictures are to be returned to me on condition that they are never shown again in England, but sent away to me on the Continent, that they may never pollute that island of lily-livered angels again. What hypocrisy and poltroonery, and how I detest and despise my England. I had rather be a German or anything than belong to such a nation of craven, cowardly hypocrites. My curse on them! They will burn my four picture books, will they? So it is decreed. But they shall burn through the thread of their own existence as a nation, at the same time. Delenda est Cartago!—but she will destroy herself, amply. Che nuoia!

Your mother says we are to stay here till the middle of September. I hope not. We have been here a month on Thursday, and when the heissgeliebte Annie is here we shall surely be a superfluity. I should like to move in another week or ten days. Shall we come to Bavaria, to Rottach, do you think? or best go south to Lugano?

I wonder if Hans is setting off across the mountains?

We are going to tea with some Taormina friends, Americans, who are staying in the Stephanie. Your mother says: Du wirst was Schönes sehen, das Stephanie!—It is all I can do not to make a really rude remark. I am so sick of all those old lies. It is terrible to be old, one becomes a bottle of old, but never *mellow lies—lies, lies, lies! everything. Weisheit der Alten!—nineteenth century lies.*

Well, I hope it's pleasant in Irschenhausen. Only today I threw away the flowers I gathered when you were here—and the toadflax (wilde Löwenmäule) were still fresh.

D. H. L.

Remember me to Alfred, and Hans—and is Marianne better?

LÖWEN
LICHTENTAL
BADEN-BADEN
21 AUGUST 1929

Dear Else:

Frieda says she wants to stay till Sunday, to have her bath and her masseuse once more. She is still troubled about the foot, though it is much better.—So I suppose we shall arrive in München on Sunday evening.—Max Mohr says he will meet us at Rottach station with a Wagen—and he knows of a nice little house for us. So it sounds quite good, if only it will not rain.

Your mother is going back into the Stift today—very sad—and Annie is going to her tomorrow. I am very fed up with here, and shall be glad to be gone too.

So—we shall see you one of these days in Bavaria!

D. H. L.

HOTEL LÖWEN
MONDAY

Dear Else:

Just a line to say we expect to leave here for München next Saturday.—I have written to Max Mohr to say we shall arrive in Rottach either on Sunday or Monday. I suppose we shall stay one night in München. What is the name of the hotel where we stayed last time? at the station?

Marianne sounded quite sad in her letter to Frieda. I'm so sorry, and do hope she's feeling better.

The Hinkes arrived on Saturday, both very nice. They are staying in the Löwen here—your mother too—she would not go back to the Stift. But Hinke returns to Völklingen today, and Annie and your mother return to the Stift on Thursday—so we want to depart on Saturday. I want to go—I get really depressed here—and you know it isn't usual for me to get depressed. But here I get spells of hopeless feeling, heavy, and I hate it. What is it? I never have them in other countries. Is it Germany? or your mother, who is now so afraid of death? Anyhow I hate it, and want to go away.

So I expect we shall see you in Bavaria—perhaps even in München. I'm so glad you are having a good time.—I can just see the yellow Pfifferlinge in the woods.

Regards to Alfred and to Marianne.—It has begun to rain again here!

D. H. L.

Villa Beau Soleil
Bandol, Var
France
4 October 1929

Dear Else:

Here we are already in a house of our own, a nice little bungalow villa right on the sea—and with bathroom and all conveniences—and a nice woman to cook and clean. It is very easy and I like it. I still love the Mediterranean, it still seems young as Odysseus, in the morning. And Frieda is happy. The only trouble is my health, which is not very good. For some reason, which I don't understand, I lost a lot of strength in Germany. I believe Germany would kill me, if I had to stay long in it. Now it has killed Stresemann—whom will it not kill?—everybody except the Hindenburgs and the old women in the Stifts. Those ancient ones are the terrible fungi, parasites of the younger life.

It is very lovely, the wind, the clouds, the running sea that bursts up like blossom on the island opposite. If only I was well, and had my strength back!

But I am so weak. And something inside me weeps black tears. I wish it would go away.

Max Mohr is quite near in the Goelands Hotel—always very nice and willing to do everything he can to help. But also his voice says the same thing over and over again: Alles ist nichts? Why must everybody say it?—when it is only they *who are nothing, and perhaps not even they. When the morning comes, and the sea runs silvery and the distant islands are delicate and clear, then I feel again, only man is vile. But man, at the moment, is very vile.*

Perhaps a woman, Francesca Ewald, whose husband is brother of the Salem Ewald woman, will write to you about translating some short story of mine. Do advise her all you can.

The Huxleys say they want to come, and take a house here. I rather hope they won't. The Brewsters also may come for the winter—their girl is in school in England.

I do hope Marianne is well from her Ischias, and that everything goes pleasantly. Frieda's foot is nearly *better—still a little stiffness.*

Ever

D. H. L.

Beau Soleil
Bandol, Var
France
14 December 1929

Dear Else:

I got a copy of "Plumed Serpent" and tried to translate a hymn—but you might as well ask me to translate into Hottentot—I can't even begin. *So that's that. I think Tal of Vienna is going to do "Lady C."—and the translator Herbert E. Herlitschka, Wiedner Gürtel 6, Wien IV, has written me several times. He seems a competent and experienced translator—and his criticism of the translation of "Women in Love" made my blood feel chill. He says he would be glad to help you with "Plumed Serpent," if there is any difficulty, or to go over the manuscript if you could send him a carbon copy. You must please yourself about it.*

You are coming to see us in the New Year. I wish you would send an approximate date, as my sister Ada also wants to come, and Barby. There's only one little extra bedroom.

We've had lovely sunny weather all week—today is a most beautiful day, still and sunny. The narcissus are in full flower in the tiny field next to us. So yellow.

My health has been a great nuisance—not so good as last winter—and it wearies me. Then I don't want to do anything.

The Brewsters are still in the hotel—and Mr. and Mrs. Di Chiara from Capri (she is American) and Ida Rauh (Mrs. Max Eastman—the socialist's wife) from Santa Fe—and they all come trooping along, so we are by no means alone. Frieda loves her little house—though it's very commonplace—but it is sunny and warm and easy, so one doesn't grumble. Her foot still troubles her a bit.

Have you seen Dr. Osborne's translation of "Fantasia"?—quite good, in my opinion.

I shall write again directly.

Love.

D. H. L.

BEAU SOLEIL
BANDOL, VAR
30 JANUARY 1930

Dear Else:

So you got back safely—at least as far as Strassburg. Here all is the same—I lay out today in the mouth of the garage, because the mistral is blowing—a sunny, brilliant day with blue sea and sharp white foam.

Barby helps Frieda to look after me, and all goes very well. Yesterday the bronchitis was much *better, but today it is tiresome again—probably the wind.*

The doctor sent word about the nursing home at Vence—it is not much of a place—like a little hotel or convalescent home. If I make good progress here, I shall not go to Vence—but if I don't get better, I will. But truly, I am already much stronger for this rest.

It was very kind of you to come all that long way to give us a helping hand—it did Frieda a lot of good, to share the responsibility with you, and I was glad to see you.

I have asked for a copy of "The Escaped Cock" for you. Barby is still in an unhappy state, inside herself. Oh dear!

Remember me to Friedel.

D. H. L.

Nearing the End

Now I am nearing the end . . . I think of Bandol and our little villa "Beau Soleil" on the sea, the big balcony windows looking toward the sea, another window at the side overlooking a field of yellow narcissus called "soleil" and pine-trees beyond and again the sea. I remember sunny days when the waves came flying along with white manes, they looked as if they might come flying right up the terrace into his room. There were plants in his room and they flowered so well and I said to him: "Why, oh why, can't you flourish like those?" I remember what a beautiful and strange time it was. One day a cat, a big handsome yellow-and-white cat came in; Lawrence chased it away. "We don't want it. If we go away it'll be miserable. We don't want to take the responsibility for it"; but the cat stayed, it insisted on it. Its name was "Micky" and it grew more and more beautiful and never a cat played more intelligently than Micky . . . he played hide-and-go-seek with me, and Lawrence played mouse with him. . . . Lawrence was such a convincing mouse . . . and then he insisted: "You must put this cat out at night or it will become a bourgeois, unbeautiful cat." So very sadly, at nightfall, in spite of Micky's remonstrances I put him out into the garden. To Mme. Martens, the cook, Lawrence said: "Vous lui donnez à manger, il dort avec moi, et Madame l'amuse."

But in the morning at dawn Micky and I appeared in Lawrence's room . . . Micky took a flying leap on to Lawrence's bed and began playing with his toes, and I looked at Lawrence to see how he was . . . his worst time was before dawn when he coughed so much, and I knew what he had been through. . . . But then at dawn I believe he felt grateful that another day had been given him. "Come when the sun rises," he said, and when I came he was glad, so very glad, as if he would say: "See, another day is given me."

The sun rose magnificently opposite his bed in red and gold across the bay and the fishermen standing up in their boats looked like eternal mythological figures dark and alive against the lit-up splendour of the sea and sky, and when I asked him: "What kind of a night did you have?" to comfort me, he would answer: "Not so bad . . ." but it was bad enough to break one's heart. . . . And his courage and unflinching spirit, doing their level best to live as long as he possibly could in this world he loved so much, gave me courage too. Never, in all illness and suffering, did he let the days sink to a dreary or dull or sordid level . . . those last months had the glamour of a rosy sunset . . . I can only think with awe of those last days of his, as of the rays of the setting sun . . . and the setting sun obliterates all the sordid details of a landscape. So the dreary passages in our lives were wiped out and he said to me: "Why, oh why did we quarrel so much?" and I could see how it grieved him . . . our terrible quarrels . . . but I answered: "Such as we were, violent creatures, how could we help it?"

One day the charming old mother of Mme. Douillet who was at the Hôtel Beau Rivage brought us two gold-fish in a bowl; "Pour amuser Monsieur," but, alas, Micky thought it was "pour amuser Monsieur le chat." With that fixed, incomprehensible cat-stare he watched those red lines moving in the bowl . . . then my life became an anxious one . . . the gold-fish had to go in the bathroom on a little table in the sun. Every morning their water was renewed and I had to let it run for half an hour into the bowl. That was all they got, the gold-fish, no food. And they flourished. . . . "Everything flourishes," I said to Lawrence imploringly, "plants and cats and gold-fish, why can't you?" And he said: "I want to, I want to, I wish I could."

His friend Earl Brewster came and massaged him every day with coconut oil . . . and it grieved me to see Lawrence's strong, straight, quick legs gone so thin, so thin . . . and one day he said to me: "I could always trust your instinct to know the right thing for me, but now you don't seem to know any more . . ." I didn't . . . I didn't know any more . . .

And one night he asked me: "Sleep with me," and I did . . . all night I was aware of his aching inflexible chest, and all night he must have been so sadly aware of my healthy body beside him . . . always before, when I slept by the side of him, I could comfort and ease him . . . now no more. . . . He was falling away from life and me, and with all my strength I was helpless. . . .

Micky had his eye on the gold-fish. One sad evening at tea-time the bathroom door was left open. . . . I came and found both gold-fish on the floor, Micky had fished them out of the bowl. I put them in quickly, one revived, a little sadder and less golden for his experience but the other was dead. Lawrence was furious with Micky. "He knew we wanted him to leave those gold-fish alone, he knew it. We feed him, we take care of him, he had no right to do it."

When I argued that it was the nature of cats and they must follow their instincts he turned on me and said: "It's your fault, you spoil him, if he wanted to eat *me* you would let him." And he wouldn't let Micky come near him for several days.

I felt: "Now I can do no more for Lawrence, only the sun and the sea and the stars and the moon at night, that's his portion now. . . ." He never would have the shutters shut or the curtains drawn, so that at night he could see the sky. In those days he wrote his "Apocalypse"; he read it to me, and how strong his voice still was, and I said: "But this is splendid."

I was reading the New Testament and told Lawrence: "I get such a kick out of it, just the same as when Azul gallops like the wind across the desert with me."

As he read it to me he got angry with all those mixed-up symbols and impossible pictures.

He said: "In this book I want to go back to old days, pre-Bible days, and pick up for us there what men felt like and lived by then."

The pure artist in him revolted! His sense of the fitness of things never left him in the lurch! He stuck to his sense of measure and I am often amused at the criticism people bring against him . . . criticisms only reveal the criticizers and their limitations. . . . If the criticizer is an interesting person his criticism will be interesting, if he isn't then it's waste of time to listen to him. If he voices a general opinion he is uninteresting too, because we all know the general opinion ad nauseam. "My flesh grows weary on my bones" was one of Lawrence's expressions when somebody held forth to him, as if one didn't know beforehand what most people will say!

One day Lawrence said to himself: "I shan't die . . . a rich man now . . . perhaps it's just as well, it might have done something to me." But I doubt whether even a million or two would have changed him!

One day he said: "I can't die, I can't die, I hate them too much! I have given too much and what did I get in return?"

It sounded so comical the way he said it, and I ignored the depth of sadness and bitterness of the words and said: "No, Lawrence, you don't hate them as much as all that." It seemed to comfort him.

And now I wonder and am grateful for the superhuman strength that was given us both in those days. Deep down I knew "something is going to happen, we are steering towards some end" but every nerve was strained and every thought and every feeling. . . . Life had to be kept going gaily at any price.

Since Doctor Max Mohr had gone, we had no doctor, only Mme. Martens, the cook. She was very good at all kinds of tisanes and inhalations and mustard plasters, and she was a very good cook.

My only grief was that we had no open fireplaces, only central heating and, thank goodness, the sun all day. Lawrence made such wonderful efforts of will to go for walks and the strain of it made him irritable. If I went with him it was pure agony walking to the corner of the little road by the sea, only a few yards! How gallantly he tried to get better and live! He was so very clever with his frail failing body. Again one could learn from him how to handle this complicated body of ours, he knew so well what was good for him, what he needed, by an unfailing instinct, or he would have died many years ago . . . and I wanted to keep him alive at any cost. I had to see him day by day getting nearer to the end, his spirit so alive and powerful that the end and death seemed unthinkable and always will be, for me.

And then Gertler sent a doctor friend to us, and when he saw Lawrence he said the only salvation was a sanatorium higher up. . . .

For the last years I had found that for a time mountain air, and then a change by the sea, seemed to suit Lawrence best. Lawrence had always thought with horror of a sanatorium, we both thought with loathing of it. Freedom that he cherished so much! He never felt like an invalid, I saw to that! Never should he feel a poor sick thing as long as I was there and his spirit! Now we had to give in . . . we were beaten. With a set face Lawrence made me bring all his papers on to his bed and he tore most of them up and made everything tidy and neat and helped to pack his own trunks, and I never cried. . . . His self-discipline kept me up, and my admiration for his unfailing courage. And the day came that the motor stood at the door of our little house, Beau Soleil. . . . Micky the cat had been taken by Achsah Brewster. She came before we started with armfuls of almond blossoms, and Earl Brewster travelled with us. . . . And patiently, with a desperate silence, Lawrence set out on his last journey. At Toulon station he had to walk down and up stairs, wasting strength he could ill afford to waste, and the shaking train and then the long drive from Antibes to the "Ad Astra" at Vence. . . . And again he had to climb stairs. There he lay in a blue room with yellow curtains and great open windows and a balcony looking over the sea. When the doctors examined him and asked him questions about himself he told them: "I have had bronchitis since I was a fortnight old."

In spite of his thinness and his illness he never lost his dignity, he fought on and he never lost hope. Friends brought flowers, pink and red cyclamen and hyacinths and fruit . . . but he suffered much and when I bade him "good night" he said: "Now I shall have to fight several battles of Waterloo before morning." I dared not understand to the full the meaning of his words. One day he said to my daughter:

"Your mother does not care for me any more, the death in me is repellent to her."

But it was the sadness of his suffering . . . and he would not eat and he had much pain . . . and we tried so hard to think of different foods for him. His friends tried to help him, the Di Chiaras and the Brewsters and Aldous and Maria Huxley and Ida Rauh.

Wells came to see him, and the Aga Khan with his charming wife. Jo Davidson did a bust of him.

One night I saw how he did not want me to go away, so I came again after dinner and I said: "I'll sleep in your room tonight." His eyes were so grateful and bright, but he turned to my daughter and said: "It isn't often I want your mother, but I do want her tonight to stay." I slept on the long chair in his room, and I looked out at the dark night and I wanted one single star to shine and comfort me, but there wasn't one; it was a dark big sky, and no moon and no stars. I knew how Lawrence suffered and yet I could not help him. So the days went by in agony and the nights too; my legs would hardly carry me, I could not stay away from him, and always the dread, "How shall I find him?" One night I thought of the occasion long ago when I knew I loved him, when a tenderness for him rose in me that I had not known before. He had taken my two little girls and me for a walk in Sherwood

Forest, through some fields we walked, and the children ran all over the place, and we came to a brook . . . it ran rather fast under a small stone bridge. The children were thrilled, the brook ran so fast. Lawrence quite forgot me but picked daisies and put them face upwards on one side of the bridge in the water and then said: "Now look, look if they come out on the other side."

He also made them paper boats and put burning matches into them; "this is the Spanish Armada, and you don't know what that was." "Yes, we do," the older girl said promptly. I can see him now, crouching down, so intent on the game, so young and quick, and the small girls in their pink and white striped Viyella frocks, long-legged like colts, in wild excitement over such a play-fellow. But that was long ago . . . and I thought: "This is the man whom they call sex-obsessed."

I slept on his cane chair several nights. I heard coughing from many rooms, old coughing and young coughing. Next to his room was a young girl with her mother, and I heard her call out: "Mama, Mama, je souffre tant!" I was glad Lawrence was a little deaf and could not hear it all. One day he tried to console me and said: "You must not feel so sympathetic for people. When people are ill or have lost their eyesight there is always a compensation. The state they are in is different. You needn't think it's the same as when you are well."

After one night when he had suffered so much, I told myself: "It is enough, it is enough; nobody should have to stand this."

He was very irritable and said: "Your sleeping here does me no good." I ran away and wept. When I came back he said so tenderly: "Don't mind, you know I want nothing but you, but sometimes something is stronger in me."

We prepared to take him out of the nursing home and rented a villa where we took him. . . . It was the only time he allowed me to put on his shoes, everything else he always did for himself. He went in the shaking taxi and he was taken into the house and lay down on the bed on which he was to die, exhausted. I slept on the couch where he could see me. He still ate. The next day was a Sunday. "Don't leave me," he said, "don't go away." So I sat by his bed and read. He was reading the life of Columbus. After lunch he began to suffer very much and about tea-time he said: "I must have a temperature, I am delirious. Give me the thermometer." This is the only time, seeing his tortured face, that I cried, and he said: "Don't cry," in a quick, compelling voice. So I ceased to cry any more. He called Aldous and Maria Huxley who were there, and for the first time he cried out to them in his agony. "I ought to have some morphine now," he told me and my daughter, so Aldous went off to find a doctor to give him some. . . . Then he said: "Hold me, hold me, I don't know where I am, I don't know where my hands are . . . where am I?"

Then the doctor came and gave him a morphine injection. After a little while he said: "I am better now, if I could only sweat I would be better . . ." and then again: "I am better now." The minutes went by, Maria Huxley was in the room with me. I held his left ankle from time to time, it felt so full of life, all my days I shall hold his ankle in my hand.

He was breathing more peacefully, and then suddenly there were gaps in the breathing. The moment came when the thread of life tore in his heaving chest, his face changed, his cheeks and jaw sank, and death had taken hold of him. . . . Death was there, Lawrence was dead. So simple, so small a change, yet so final, so staggering. Death!

I walked up and down beside his room, by the balcony, and everything looked different, there was a new thing, death, where there had been life, such intense life. The olive trees outside looked so black and close, and the sky so near; I looked into the room, there were his slippers with the shape of his feet standing neatly under the bed, and under the sheet he lay, cold and remote, he whose ankle I had held alive only an hour or so ago. . . . I looked at his face. So proud, manly and splendid he looked, a new face there was. All suffering had been wiped from it, it was as if I had never seen him or known him in all the completeness of his being. I wanted to touch him but dared not, he was no longer in life with me. There had been the change, he belonged somewhere else now, to all the elements; he was the earth and sky, but no longer a living man. Lawrence, my Lorenzo who had loved me and I him . . . he was dead. . . .

Then we buried him, very simply, like a bird we put him away, a few of us who loved him. We put flowers into his grave and all I said was: "Good-bye, Lorenzo," as his friends and I put lots and lots of mimosa on his coffin. Then he was covered over with earth while the sun came out on to his small grave in the little cemetery of Vence which looks over the Mediterranean that he cared for so much.

Conclusion

Now THAT I have told my story in such a condensed way, letting blow through my mind anything that wanted to blow, I know how little I have said—how much I could say that perhaps would be more interesting.

But I wrote what rose up, and here it it.

FRIEDA LAWRENCE

Kiowa Ranch
San Cristobal
New Mexico